S0-CJO-328

# DATE DUE

| | | | |
|---|---|---|---|
| | | | |
| | | | |
| | | | |
| | | | |
| '76 | | | |
| | | | |
| | | | |
| | | | |
| | | | |
| | | | |
| | | | |
| | | | |
| | | | |
| | | | |
| | | | |
| | | | |
| | | | |
| | | | |
| GAYLORD | | | PRINTED IN U.S.A. |

PLYMOUTH HIGH SCHOOL LIBRARY

# The Kennedy Brothers

*About the Book*

No political dynasty in American history has been more fascinating than that of the Kennedys of Massachusetts. Dramatically and searchingly, author Alfred Steinberg tells here the story of four brothers who linked their destinies to the destiny of their country. Three died while serving the United States of America—Joseph, Jr., as a flier in World War II, John felled by an assassin's bullet when President, Robert by another assassin when he was a U.S. Senator seeking the Presidency. What does the future hold for Senator Edward Kennedy? Steinberg shows how behind the ambitions of all the sons stood a wealthy, brilliant father who trained his boys for the Presidency.

*LIVES TO*  *REMEMBER*

# THE
# Kennedy
# Brothers

PLYMOUTH HIGH SCHOOL LIBRARY

by
ALFRED
STEINBERG

*G. P. Putnam's Sons*
*New York*

To Rose Kennedy
and her unconquerable spirit

Second Impression

Copyright © 1969 by Alfred Steinberg
All rights reserved. Published simultaneously in the Dominion of Canada
by Longmans Canada Limited, Toronto.
Library of Congress Catalog Card Number: 74-75596
PRINTED IN THE UNITED STATES OF AMERICA
12 up

# Contents

*LIVES TO REMEMBER* is a series of concise biographies introducing the world's great men and women.

One of the groups is famed Americans, who include:

# The Kennedy Brothers

# 1 The Kennedy Clan

When the Founding Fathers wrote the Constitution of the United States in 1787, there seemed little likelihood that political dynasties might develop. In a country without a hereditary monarchy, they agreed, national power could not be passed on from one member of a governing family to another.

Yet since that time, several American families have appeared destined to form political dynasties. The first was the Adams clan, headed by John Adams of Massachusetts. After a long and distinguished career as a Revolutionary War patriot, legislator, and diplomat, John Adams served as Vice President under George Washington before succeeding him in 1797. Next up the Adams ladder of national power was John Quincy Adams, his son, who occupied the White House from 1825 to 1829 as the sixth American President. Charles Francis Adams, in the next generation, was a Congressman and a Vice Presidential nominee. Two generations later, another Charles Francis Adams served as Secretary of the Navy in the Cabinet of Herbert Hoover.

For a time in the nineteenth century, Americans expected John Van Buren, son of Martin Van Buren, to win the Presidency on his own after his father left the White House in 1841. Editors argued that if the short, stout father, who spoke with a lisp and a trace of a Dutch accent, could be President, why not the son who was tall, handsome, and an excellent speaker? Yet although Prince John, as he was called, helped organize the Free-Soil Party in 1848, he secured the Presidential nomination for his father, then seven years out of office, instead of for himself.

Still another candidate for an American political dynasty was the highly successful Harrison family. Benjamin Harrison was an early Virginia patriot, a member of the Continental Congress, and a signer of the Declaration of Independence. The youngest of his seven children was William Henry Harrison, a hero of the War of 1812 and the winner of the Presidency in 1840. In turn, William's fifth child, John Scott Harrison, served two terms in Congress, and John's fifth child, another Benjamin Harrison, served as President from 1889 to 1893.

In the first half of the twentieth century the principal American family with the potential of a political dynasty was that of Franklin Delano Roosevelt. Throughout his four elected terms, newspapers focused a great deal of attention on his four sons as his political heirs. Yet although two became Congressmen and one a mayor, a Roosevelt dynasty did not develop.

# The Kennedy Clan

Still another family in the twentieth century seemed destined for success as a dynasty. This was the Kennedy clan of Massachusetts—the four sons of Joseph Patrick Kennedy, who composed the most unusual political family in American history. Joseph Patrick Kennedy, Jr., was the oldest of the boys; John Fitzerald Kennedy was next; then came Robert Francis Kennedy; and finally Edward Moore Kennedy.

Joe, the natural leader; Jack, the aloof, restrained Kennedy; Bobby, the emotional and aggressive member of the clan; and friendly Teddy—fate was to cut short the lives of three long before their proper day in the sun.

It was the potato famine of the 1840's that brought Patrick Kennedy, the great-grandfather of the Kennedy boys, to America from Ireland. Potatoes not destroyed by blight in the fields rotted later in warehouses. Starvation and disease swept the country, and more than 2,000,000 persons fled their native land.

Among them was Patrick Kennedy, a twenty-six-year-old tenant farmer, who quit his two-room, straw-thatched, dirt-floor cottage in County Wexford to climb aboard a packet ship bound for the New World in 1849. Many of his fellow passengers jammed in the hold of the verminous vessel perished long before the six weeks' trip ended on the coast of Massachusetts.

Here on the mudflats of East Boston, Pat Kennedy found work as a barrelmaker and married Bridget Murphy. The two had four children and were raising them in the squalid Irish ghetto when the cholera epidemic of 1858 felled Pat and he died at the young age of thirty-five. His widow, left without money, ran a stationery shop for a short time, then became a hairdresser in a downtown Boston department store.

Bridget Kennedy's youngest child and only son was Patrick Joseph Kennedy, one day to be the grandfather of the four Kennedy boys. P.J., as he was generally called throughout his seventy-one years, was only a few months old when his father died. He grew up bright and alert, yet dropped out of parochial grammar school before graduation because he wanted to bring some money into the household. P.J. hoped for a clerical job, but he found that Boston newspaper want ads for beginning clerks carried the initials NINA, a shorthand warning that "No Irish Need Apply." So P.J.'s first job was as a stevedore, unloading cargo on the docks of East Boston.

Friends recognized that the round-faced young man with the handlebar mustache was too ambitious to spend his life as a stevedore. But not until his mid-twenties did P.J. find his escape from dock work. A saloon in Haymarket Square was headed for bankruptcy, and he was able to buy it without a down payment.

Hard work and P.J.'s pleasing personality soon revived the fortunes of the tavern, and it became a neighborhood center. The Irish who congregated there' liked to talk politics and discuss their troubles. Kennedy, a nondrinker, gave them his quiet opinions and also gained a reputation for having a kind heart. Many a bushel of coal and basket of food went to families of unemployed Irishmen, thanks to his charity. He also kept track of available jobs and sent dozens of persons off to fill them.

Within a year, P.J.'s customers in his saloon were telling him he was just the man they needed to represent their interests and run their political ward. P.J. agreed,

and in 1886, when he was twenty-eight, he ran for office
and won election to the Massachusetts House of Representatives. After serving five terms, he moved to the State
Senate in 1892, and when state service began to pall,
P.J. held a succession of local offices. For a time he was
Boston's fire commissioner, then street commissioner and
elections board chief, before he settled down to doing
what he liked best—running his ward as its political
boss. There were those who said that his only deficiency
as a politician was that his mind went blank whenever
he had to deliver a speech in public.

Shortly after his first election to the Massachusetts
House of Representatives, P.J. married Mary Hickey,
who came from a highly regarded Irish family. One of
her brothers was a doctor, another a mayor, and a third
a Boston police captain. In time, the Kennedys had three
children, the oldest of whom was their only son. This
infant, who became the father of the four Kennedy boys,
was born on September 6, 1888. P.J. wanted to name the
baby after himself, but his wife argued that he would
grow up as "Little P.J.," and she won a compromise to
reverse the names to Joseph Patrick Kennedy in order
to avoid this.

The rising fortunes of the Kennedy family were easily
noted. Baby Joe was born in a small, wooden house close
to his father's saloon on busy Meridian Street. But after
a few years the Kennedys left the muddy lowlands for a
fine house four stories high on top a hill overlooking East
Boston Harbor. The reason for this better life was that
P.J. had acquired control over three barrooms in addition to his Haymarket Square saloon. He had also become a wholesale liquor distributor, proprietor of a retail

liquor store, part owner of a coal company, and a founder of a neighborhood bank.

Despite his comfortable income, P.J. expected his son to earn his own spending money and learn the value of a dollar. So at the age of nine Joseph Kennedy could be seen peddling papers on Boston streets, lighting gas lamps and stoves for religious Jews on Saturdays, and selling candy and peanuts aboard summertime excursion boats. Still other occupations at which he worked during his youth included collecting tickets on a sightseeing boat, working as an office boy in a bank, and raising pigeons. Early in life, he set his ambition on becoming a rich man.

Joseph's education began at the local School of the Assumption. But after the seventh grade, his mother sent him to a nonparochial school, where he could meet boys from other backgrounds. The shift was to the Boston Latin School, a renowned institution founded in 1635 and numbering Benjamin Franklin and John Hancock among its earlier pupils.

One drawback of Boston Latin for Joseph was that it was far from home, and he was required to rise especially early and ride the North Ferry across the canal to the school. Another drawback was that academic standards were high and he had little interest in his classwork. He did so poorly his senior year that he was forced to repeat it.

It was chiefly the nonacademic program at Boston Latin that left him afterward with fond memories of the school. In his teens he had grown tall and muscular, and he was easily spotted on the baseball diamond by his red hair, freckled face, and the power of his bat. One year he won the Mayor's Cup for having the highest batting average among Boston's high school players. He was also the student colonel of Boston Latin's military regiment, which won first prize in citywide competition, shortly before his graduation in 1908.

After high school, Joseph might have joined his friends at either of Boston's two Catholic colleges if his mother had not long dreamed of having a son at Harvard. So he went instead to this famed university, where he majored in economics and history, worked hard at improving his baseball skills, and vowed to classmates he would be a millionaire by his thirty-fifth birthday.

Again, Joe did not prove to be a scholar, and he complained that certain social clubs were closed to him because his grandfather was an Irish immigrant. Nor did he go on European vacations as did many of his classmates. But he managed to join some respected student social organizations, and he and a partner each earned $5,000 by running tourist buses for three summers to historic Lexington and Concord.

The route Joseph planned to use to reach his goal of becoming a millionaire was the banking business, and when he was graduated from Harvard in 1912, he looked about for openings in this field. However, since Boston's downtown banks refused to employ persons of Irish descent at other than menial jobs, he was forced to settle for a job in the counting room of the small Columbia Trust Company, in which his father held an interest. But Columbia Trust had only $200,000 in deposits, and its operations were so simple that he gained little insight into the practices of what he knew must be a complex business. Finally, after several months, he asked his father to use his political influence to help him get a job as a state bank examiner.

The job paid only $30 a week, but it gave him priceless experience in the big-money market. By virtue of his title, he had a ready entrance into the behind-the-scenes activities of the oldest and most powerful banks in eastern Massachusetts, and his study of their ledgers helped him gain a sound education in the mysteries of money manipulations.

Had the large First Ward National Bank of Boston not decided to seize control of the small bank in which his father owned several thousand dollars' worth of stock, Joseph Kennedy would have remained a state bank examiner longer than a year. But First Ward National was quietly buying Columbia Trust stock from individual holders, with the intention of controlling the next annual election of officers, and P.J. asked his son to help save the bank.

Harvard friends lent $45,000 to Joseph Kennedy, and with this sum he purchased enough stock not only to defeat First Ward but also to be elected president of Columbia Trust. The fight with First Ward brought him his first newspaper attention, and when reporters learned he was at twenty-five the youngest bank president in the United States, additional newspaper stories followed. One Boston paper described him as "a direct action man who works in rolled-up sleeves, lunching on milk and crackers."

Only months after he became a bank president in 1914, another major change occurred in his life. This was his marriage to Rose Fitzgerald, daughter of Boston's colorful politician John Francis Fitzgerald.

A short, talkative man, Fitzgerald had gone much further in politics than his friend and competitor, P.J. Kennedy, after just as humble a start. His father, too, had come from County Wexford, Ireland, during the potato famine, but instead of settling in East Boston as had Pat Kennedy, Tom Fitzgerald had begun his American existence in the North End slum section of Boston. Here he acquired a combination liquor-grocery store near the century-old home of Paul Revere, married Rose Mary Murray, and reared a large family in an eight-family tenement house close by the scene of the Boston Tea Party of 1773.

John F. Fitzgerald was the third of their seven sons. Born in 1863, in the midst of the Civil War, he possessed a happy, bubbling personality that seldom failed him. In appearance, he bore a striking resemblance to his hero Napoleon Bonaparte, and fellow students at Boston Latin School dubbed him Little Napoleon. Later on, he was also called Fitzie and Little Johnny Fitz and, finally, Honey Fitz, the nickname by which he was known the rest of his life.

Despite the death of his mother in 1878 when he was fifteen, Honey Fitz continued with his schooling. However, when his father died of pneumonia three years later, he was forced to quit Harvard Medical School in his freshman year and find a job.

For five years, Honey Fitz worked as a clerk in the Boston customhouse before going into the profitable insurance business. By his mid-twenties Honey Fitz was developing a taste for political power and public office.

Through hard work and intrigue, he became a ward boss like P.J. Kennedy, and in 1892 he won a seat on the Boston Common Council. A year later he was elected to the State Senate; then, in 1894, he ran and won a seat in the U.S. House of Representatives, where he served three terms in Washington.

Honey Fitz would have liked a fourth term, but Martin "The Mahatma" Lomasney, the city boss, decided that Joseph Aloysius Conry, head of the Board of Aldermen, should have a chance to hobnob with Presidents and other national figures. This left Honey Fitz with no alternative, and he retired from Congress when his term expired in 1901.

However, once back in Massachusetts, he grew quickly dissatisfied with returning to his old post as "the little Napoleon of the Sixth Ward." Despite the fact that he had moved to the suburbs, Honey Fitz now set his sights on becoming mayor of Boston. This was a goal The Mahatma also firmly opposed, and Honey Fitz was involved in five years of intensive daily effort before success came.

Hardly a week passed without at least a dozen street-corner rallies at which Honey Fitz delivered a peppy speech promising a "bigger, better, busier Boston." He spoke rapidly, shouting every third or fourth word for emphasis, and all of it came out in a rich Irish brogue. In addition, no Honey Fitz rally was complete without his off-key rendition of "Sweet Adeline" and his stiff-legged Irish jig.

Other campaign activities involved attending hundreds of weddings and wakes. At the happy ceremonies, he kissed the bride and toasted the young couple with

# 2 Joseph Patrick Kennedy, Jr.

To AVOID Boston's hot months in 1915, Joseph and Rose Kennedy drove to Hull, a resort village on the shore of Nantasket Bay, to spend the summer at her parents' cottage. It was here on July 25 that the local doctor was hurriedly summoned, and Mrs. Kennedy gave birth to the first of her nine children. She and her husband had decided in advance to name the expected baby after themselves—either Joseph or Rose—and when the infant was a boy, he was christened Joseph Patrick Kennedy, Jr.

With his blue eyes and square face, Little Joe, as he was immediately nicknamed, bore a strong resemblance both to his mother and to his grandfather Honey Fitz. He was also a healthy and happy baby, yet his father was involved in so many outside activities that he could not concentrate on the joys of parenthood.

Joseph Kennedy, the young bank president, was still

heavily in debt, and he had gone into the real estate business on the side for extra income. In addition, he was being pushed into service as a chauffeur and campaign meeting arranger by Honey Fitz, who had decided to run in 1916 for the U.S. Senate seat of Senator Henry Cabot Lodge. Joseph Kennedy's state of mind was revealed one winter day when he and Edward Moore, Honey Fitz's secretary, went for a walk and talk, pulling Little Joe on a homemade sled behind them. After they had walked a long distance, Moore glanced back and discovered the sled was empty. They raced back along their route with mounting concern until they came upon the baby lying in the snow. Little Joe had a happy smile on his cold face.

Honey Fitz had not bothered to run before for the Senate because Senators had been chosen by the state legislature, and small, frail, goateed Lodge, with a PhD from Harvard and as a member of an old and wealthy Yankee family, had too many friends in the statehouse who considered him with awe. But the Seventeenth Amendment to the Constitution was now law, and it required that the people elect Senators. On this basis, Honey Fitz believed he had a better chance in the Bay State than Lodge.

Joseph Kennedy was pressed into daily service as the campaign between his father-in-law and Lodge reached fever pitch. He listened to "Sweet Adeline" a dozen times a day along with repeated jokes and stories, and he felt the disappointment of the candidate when President Woodrow Wilson refused to support him, even though both were Democrats. Honey Fitz had called for American aid to Ireland in her fight for independence from Great Britain, but with the British Empire then engaged in a war against the German Kaiser, Wilson considered this an untimely demand.

Local politicians said that had Wilson endorsed Honey Fitz, the President would have gained the Irish vote and would also have enabled Honey Fitz to pick up some non-Irish support. But this was not the case, and Wilson lost Massachusetts by 20,000 votes, while Honey Fitz lost by only 33,000 votes out of 500,000 ballots cast. The disaster to Wilson was that Lodge remained in the Senate, where eventually he prevented the necessary approval of the League of Nations.

In May, 1917, Rose Kennedy had her second son, and she named him John Fitzgerald Kennedy after her father. By now the United States was at war with Germany, and Joseph Kennedy was working as the $20,000-a-year assistant general manager of the Bethlehem Steel Company's shipyard near Quincy, where battleships, destroyers, and submarines were produced.

He also entered a highly profitable venture after listening to some of the 40,000 shipyard workers grumble because there were no restaurants in the area. With Bethlehem's permission, he opened his Victory Luncheon and earned so much money that after the war ended he was able to finance the purchase of thirty-nine movie theaters. In addition, he became the manager of a stockbroker's Boston branch in order to learn the secrets of that big-money business.

All these activities kept him so busy that he could spend little time with his growing family. Besides Little Joe and Jack, there were Rosemary, born in 1918, Kathleen (Kick), in 1920, and Eunice, in 1921. "She was the glue" was how her son Jack once described Rose

Kennedy's vital role in managing the family during his early years.

Mrs. Kennedy employed governesses for the older children and nurses for the younger. A large staff of servants cared for the twelve-room house in Brookline to which Kennedy had moved his family; a chauffeur and Rolls-Royce were on hand for transportation. Nevertheless, Mrs. Kennedy put in a full day with her children. This was part of her husband's philosophy that only through "togetherness" could an outstanding family come about. "We decided that our children were going to be our best friends," said Rose Kennedy, "and we could never see too much of them. It was better to bring up our family than go out to dinner."

As a result, she said, "On pleasant days I took the children for walks. I wheeled one in a baby carriage and two or three toddled along with me. I also made it a point each day to take them into church for a visit." She was a strict disciplinarian: "I used to have a ruler around, and paddled them occasionally, because when they're young that's all they understand." From the start she kept complete records for each child, noting illnesses, visits to doctors and dentists, and treatment, and so that they would not "knock each other down or gouge each other in the eyes with toys," she built wooden folding partitions on the wide front porch to form separate playrooms.

If Mrs. Kennedy was the glue that held the family together in those early years, Little Joe contributed a great deal to her success. It was to him that she turned to act as a substitute father for his younger brothers and sisters. This was a role he continued throughout his life. "Joe did many things well," Jack later recalled his brother's im-

portant family role, "but I have always felt that Joe achieved his greatest success as the older brother.

"Very early in life he acquired a sense of responsibility toward his brothers and sisters, and I do not think he ever forgot it. Toward me, who was nearly his own age, his responsibility consisted in setting a standard that was uniformly high. . . . He would spend long hours throwing a football with Bobby, swimming with Teddy and teaching the younger girls how to sail. He made the task of bringing up a large family immeasurably easier for my father and mother, for what they taught him he passed on to us."

Little Joe's role as group leader for the younger Kennedys began about the time he started school. "Their mother insisted that the girls go to Catholic schools," said Joseph Kennedy. "I had other ideas for the boys' schooling. I figured the boys could get all the religion they needed in church, and that it would be broadening for them to attend Protestant schools."

Joe started at the Dexter Academy in 1921. This was a private school located only a few blocks from the Kennedy home, and it was chosen both for its non-Catholic direction and for the fact that Joe could come home each day.

It took Joe only a few years before he dominated his classmates just as he did his younger brothers and sisters. His teachers found him quick and bright in class and the school's outstanding athlete on the playground. But this picture of the model youngster differed sharply from the one drawn of him in church. The priest saw him as a mischievous lad full of pranks, while the nuns who taught him in Sunday school called Joe a boy "who couldn't pass a hat without squashing it or leave an unprotected shin unkicked. He was cracked on the head so often it was a wonder the top of his head wasn't flatter than a pancake."

Yet he changed back to his mother's assistant on returning home. "If you bring up the older children so they do things in a good way and give them a lot of attention," his mother said proudly, "the younger ones are great imitators and will follow the older ones' example."

His sister Kathleen, or Kick, as she was called, said that she "often looked upon Joe with something closely akin to awe. Younger brothers and sisters regarded him as the foundation stone of the family, and that is the way we all unconsciously regarded Joe."

When one of the younger girls misbehaved, Joe would ask Kick to take her aside and lecture her. He was especially kind to sister Rosemary, three years his junior, who was being reared at home, though mentally retarded. At first he included her in games; when she grew steadily less physically and mentally adept, he kept careful watch on her outdoors so that she would not harm herself.

Joe was far more strict and direct in dealing with his brothers. Teddy Kennedy, almost seventeen years his junior, was twelve years old when he put on paper the method Joe used to punish him for a sailing mistake. Teddy wrote that when he was only five, he had been Joe's partner in a sailboat contest and he aroused Joe's anger because he did not understand sailing terms. The next thing he knew, he wrote, Joe "zeized me by the pants and through me into the cold water. I was scared to death practully. I then heard a splash and I felt his hand grab my shirt and then he lifted me into the boat

28

We continued the race and came in second. One falt Joe had was he got very easily mad in a race as you have witnessed."

Of his eight brothers and sisters, there was one who refused to carry out Joe's orders. This was Jack, with whom he shared a bedroom in the big house in Brookline. Unfortunately for Jack, two years his junior, Joe was husky and tall, while Jack was a sickly child and painfully thin. But this physical difference did not keep him from challenging Joe at every order.

"Joe had a pugnacious personality," Jack once said, blaming his older brother for their troubles. "Later on it smoothed out, but it was a problem in my boyhood."

Bobby Kennedy remembered one occasion when he and the other young Kennedys cowered on the stairway in fright while Joe and Jack wrestled savagely on the living-room rug. Like all other battles, this one ended with Joe's pinning Jack's shoulders to the floor. Jack was forever challenging Joe to races, and Bobby remembered when his older brothers engaged in a bicycle race around the block. They set off in opposite directions, and on meeting on the far side of the block, they rammed their bikes head on. Joe fell uninjured, while Jack required twenty-eight stitches.

The entire family once witnessed a controversial scene between the two boys. The Kennedys were in the dining room of their beach place, and servants had just placed their desserts before them. Jack finished his chocolate cream pie in a hurry, then snatched Joe's piece off his plate and pushed it into his own mouth. Jack ran from the dining room with Joe in swift pursuit and the rest of the family following the two toward the ocean breakwater.

Trapped on the ledge, Jack cupped his hands to dive fully clothed into the sea. But Joe pulled him back and then doubled up with laughter at the sight of his terrified brother whose face was crusted with whipped cream.

Joseph Kennedy's view of the fights between Joe and Jack was that such rivalry was commonplace between brothers close in years. Moreover, he observed that at the end of every squabble Jack immediately forgot it and was Joe's friend once more. His conclusion was that so long as they fought as a unit against outsiders, he would ignore their personal troubles.

In contrast with his position was that of his wife. When her husband was away and the boys argued or fought, she sent them to their room and restricted them to a bread-and-water dinner. This had the effect of drawing her sons together, and after a short stay in their room they would tiptoe down the backstairs to the kitchen, where the good-hearted Irish cook let them raid the icebox. Sometimes Mrs. Kennedy punished them by cutting off their next week's allowance, but Harry Pattison, the Kennedy chauffeur, foiled her effort by slipping them his small change. "You're spoiling them!" she scolded Pattison one afternoon when she caught him flipping dimes to Joe and Jack.

From an early age, Joe and Jack were made aware of politics because of "Grampas" P.J. Kennedy and Honey Fitz. On a pleasant Sunday afternoon, Harry Pattison drove the Kennedys 10 miles to Winthrop to visit Grampa Kennedy, who lived alone since 1923, when Gramma died. Joe saw P.J. Kennedy as a tall, heavyset old man with a white, handlebar mustache who insisted that the children sit quietly until it was time to leave. "On

those Sunday afternoon visits," Jack later recalled, "Grampa wouldn't let us cut up or even wink in his presence."

Although he was long out of politics, this was P.J.'s continuing interest, and he and his son talked for hours about his past experiences. One time Joseph Kennedy turned to Little Joe and told him that his earliest political memory was of a visit two ward heelers made to his father's house on election day. "Pat," one said proudly, "we voted one hundred and twenty-eight times today."

Unlike P.J., Grampa Honey Fitz still had dreams of future political successes, and he treated his two oldest grandsons to a firsthand look at an active campaigner. Following his defeat by Senator Henry Cabot Lodge in 1916, Honey Fitz had run two years later for the seat in the U.S. House of Representatives then held by "Weeping" Peter Tague, the choice of the Democratic bosses. Supporters of both candidates bought votes and engaged in other dishonest tactics. Honey Fitz, who won by 238 votes, had served eight months as a Congressman when the House voted to unseat him and reinstate Tague. When Honey Fitz returned to Boston, he insisted to reporters that Tague's campaign had been far more fraudulent than his own, and he pointed out that former President William McKinley had suffered a similar temporary setback to his great career when the House ousted him for fraudulent electioneering in 1884.

By the time Little Joe was aware of Honey Fitz's chief interest it was 1922, and Grampa was running for governor against a man named Channing Cox. Honey Fitz wanted him and Jack along on his street corner campaign in Boston, and dozens of times the two boys watched him dance his stiff-legged Irish jig and sing "Sweet Adeline." The boys were also fascinated when Grampa practiced the Irish Switch. This consisted of his shaking hands with one person, while speaking to a second person and gazing warmly into the eyes of a third. In addition, the two boys served as Grampa's private audience when he rehearsed his "spontaneous" campaign speeches. But all the excitement ended one day in November, 1922, when Cox defeated Grampa by 60.000 votes and became governor.

After his defeat, Honey Fitz had more time for his grandsons. A greeting ritual developed between him and Little Joe. On sight of each other, each would shout out the seventy-one-word opening sentence of the Declaration of Independence that began: "When in the Course of human events, it becomes necessary for people to dissolve the political bonds. . . ." Following this recitation, sometimes Honey Fitz took Joe and Jack to the Franklin Park Zoo or to the Public Garden to ride in the swan boats. Occasionally he took them to Fenway Park to watch the Boston Red Sox play baseball and told them of the tragedy when the team sold its great star, Babe Ruth, to the New York Yankees.

When he was not taking the boys on outings, Honey Fitz enjoyed telling them about the Presidents he had known. The year he went to Congress, he said, Grover Cleveland lived in the White House, and the President's entire White House staff consisted of a single assistant, Robert Lincoln O'Brien. When O'Brien was on vacation, Cleveland answered his own mail in longhand. The White House had only one telephone, and it was on the

President's desk, Grampa recalled. When it rang, Cleveland answered it himself.

Grampa told the boys he had influenced Cleveland on a bill that would have barred anyone from migrating to the United States who could not read the U.S. Constitution. After Congress passed this bill, it had gone to Cleveland for his approval or veto, and when Honey Fitz learned that the President planned to sign it into law, he had hurried to the White House to explain its true purpose.

Certainly it would be admirable if all immigrants were able to read the Constitution in English, Grampa said he told Cleveland. But this bill had been specifically designed to keep out the poor and those with little or no education. In truth, his own father, Tom Fitzgerald, would have been barred, he pointed out to the President. Cleveland thanked him for his explanation and promptly vetoed the bill, added Grampa, and so the door was kept open for tens of millions of unfortunate persons.

Despite Cleveland's action, he had personally liked President McKinley better, said Grampa. McKinley was a friendlier man and had asked him to bring his daughters to the White House to visit. Rose Kennedy confirmed her father's story and gave details of the day she and her younger sister, Agnes, went to the Executive Mansion.

"President McKinley said that my seven-year-old sister was the prettiest girl who ever had visited the White House," said Rose Kennedy with pride.

But a moment later her smile faded when little Jack blurted: "Why didn't he say it to you, Mother?"

Politics and current affairs were also favorite mealtime subjects within the Kennedy household. At the dinner table, when he was home, Joseph Kennedy enjoyed lecturing on politics and political personalities. "At first they were mostly monologues," said Jack. "But we didn't have opinions in those days. Later, the discussions included us more."

For a time, only Joe was permitted to break into his father's lectures. Then Jack was allowed to speak, and finally all the children joined in. "Those discussions at dinner were never a formal thing," Mr. Kennedy once commented on his efforts at home education. "We never organized debates. They were more a discussion of personalities rather than politics."

Tempers sometimes flashed at the table. Once, when the elder Kennedy ridiculed Joe's opinion, the boy fled from the dining room in fury. Another time it was the father who left in anger. Then there was the night Joe and Jack combined forces in a political argument with their father. Afterward, when Mrs. Kennedy expressed concern, her husband said reassuringly, "I can take care of myself. The important thing is that they fight together."

On Sundays when their father was absent, the Kennedy children would read the "News of the Week in Review" section of the New York *Times*. At lunch Joe served as moderator and tested his brothers and sisters on what they had read.

Early in 1926 the Kennedys quit their Brookline home and moved to New York State. Joe was in his sixth year at Dexter Academy when he was suddenly uprooted, but the shift was made necessary because of his father's rising fortune. The elder Kennedy had become a millionaire stock market speculator; in addition to his movie theater chain, he had gained control of the Film Booking Office of America. The FBO was a major producer of low-quality Westerns and adventure movies, and it averaged one completed film a week to meet the needs of the 700 theaters it serviced. With the stock market and the head office of FBO centered in New York City, the elder Kennedy had no alternative except to move there.

So late one afternoon on a spring day in 1926 Little Joe shepherded his younger brothers and sisters aboard their father's private railroad car in Boston's South Station. A nurse carried Robert Francis "Bobby" Kennedy aboard, for he was only four months old. Then, when the parents and the corps of servants crowded into the car, the move to New York began.

Joseph Kennedy's first home in New York was a large place in Riverdale, located in Bronx County, in the north of the city. When this proved inadequate, he bought a $250,000 mansion set in five acres of well-tended lawns and gardens in nearby Bronxville, in Westchester County. Joe and Jack were enrolled in the Riverdale Country School in the West Bronx, and Mr. Kennedy again told Joe he was counting on him to help watch over the younger Kennedys.

Mrs. Kennedy made his task somewhat easier by establishing new strict rules. The children were forbidden to ride their bicycles off the estate; they had to be seated at the dining room table five minutes before mealtime; no one was to be outdoors after dark; all had to wear the same color bathing suit at the beach for instant recognition in a crowd.

But there were no rules on the intensity in which they

played games. In the thirteen years the Kennedys lived on their Bronxville estate, friends and neighbors were certain one or more Kennedys would be maimed in the touch football games played there. A friend of Joe's recalled: "There were a lot of trees around the lawn at Bronxville. I always ran looking for the trees and the ball at the same time. But Joe and Jack and later Bobby never did, and WHANG! That was that. They were always knocking themselves out. I can remember when one or the other of the boys would be picked up unconscious; they were always bandaged and bruised all over."

One of the big problems of the motion-picture industry was to determine in advance whether the public would pay to see a new actor. Joseph Kennedy relied on two advisers for guidance on many occasions—his sons Joe and Jack. For example, Red Grange, the famous football player at the University of Illinois, came to Kennedy's New York office one morning and told him he wanted to be a movie star.

Mr. Kennedy knew that several other studios had already rejected Grange, and his first thought was to do the same. However, he told Grange he would put the matter to his experts and let him know the results. That evening the elder Kennedy called eleven-year-old Joe and nine-year-old Jack into the library, closed the doors, and solemnly asked, "Would you like to see Red Grange in the movies?"

"Yes, we would!" was the shouted reply.

So the following day, Grange was hired, not knowing on whom his fate had rested.

Shortly after he settled his family in New York, Joseph Kennedy made a trip to Hollywood. He spent much of the next three years in California away from his family. Nevertheless, he took the time each summer to vacation in Massachusetts with his wife and children.

In the years before the move to New York, the Kennedys had vacationed at Cohasset Beach, about 30 miles southeast of Boston. But after Joseph Kennedy was blackballed from membership in the Cohasset Country Club, he began a search for a new summer residence. His hunt brought him in his blue Rolls-Royce to Cape Cod, and at Hyannis Port it ended with the purchase of a three-gabled, eighteen-room house with nine baths. The "cottage," as Kennedy described the house, sat on two and a half acres of land fronting on Nantucket Sound.

It was in Hyannis Port that Joseph Kennedy undertook to shape the character of his children in a most unusual fashion. He wanted to instill in them an overriding desire to win. He proposed to do this through athletic competition, believing the winning instinct would spill over into all other activities as the children grew older.

Daughter Eunice once spoke about her father's demand that they win at whatever they did. "Even when we were six and seven years old," she said, "Daddy always entered us in public swimming races, in the different age categories, so we didn't have to swim against each other. And he did the same thing with us in sailing races. And if we won, he got terribly enthusiastic. Daddy was always very competitive. The thing he always kept telling us was that coming in second was just no good. The important thing was to win—don't come in second or third —that doesn't count—but win, win, win."

Kennedy built a swimming pool and a fine tennis court on his Hyannis Port property and set aside areas for softball and touch football, and since sailboat racing was a major local interest, he decided that his children must become champion sailors. When Joe and Jack got their first sailboat in 1927, they called it the *Rose Elizabeth* in honor of their mother. Kennedy said that when the two boys went out in the boat, they were still "so small you couldn't see their heads and it looked from shore as if the boat were empty."

The boys won their first race that year, receiving publicity in Boston, thanks to Grampa Honey Fitz. When they returned to the house in triumph after winning a contest for novices, Joe caught sight of an overturned, bobbing sailboat far out in the harbor with a man clinging to it. Quickly, he and Jack leaped into their boat and rushed to the rescue.

Honey Fitz was visiting the Kennedys that day. Always on the lookout for publicity in case he ran again for office, he telephoned the editor of the Boston *Post* with the story of his grandsons' heroism. The next day's paper contained an article that began: "Joseph P. Kennedy, Jr., twelve, and Jack Fitzgerald Kennedy, ten, sons of Joseph P. Kennedy, motion picture magnate and banker, and grandsons of John F. Fitzgerald, performed a daring rescue this afternoon in Hyannis Harbor." The story went on to call the boys "champions" at sailing.

After the little *Rose Elizabeth,* there were several other boats. One was named *The Ten of Us,* but following Teddy's birth in 1932, the boat was appropriately renamed *One More.* Other Kennedy boats included the *Victura, Flash I* and *II,* the *Restovus,* and a 50-foot cruiser named *Marlin.*

Kennedy never learned the art of sailing; he depended

on Little Joe to master it and pass on his techniques to his younger brothers and sisters. Nevertheless, he was able to judge their progress by the number of races they won, and he could sense if they had done their best by the expressions on their faces when they returned to the house. "There was the devil to pay if they didn't win every race," a family friend said. The girls were expected to be as competitive as the boys, and Joe worked just as hard with them as he did with the boys. So desirous for victory was Eunice when she served as skipper in a race for juniors that before the gun sounded at the outset, her voice could be heard far back on shore: "All right, now! Everyone say a 'Hail Mary!' "

Kennedy, who sat on the porch with a clattering stock market ticker tape machine alongside him, studied the children after the races. Those who he was convinced had not performed properly were stopped and treated to severe criticism before the rest of the family. Then he or she was ordered to eat dinner in the kitchen. As a rule, the one being punished would later admit a lack of top effort and promise to do better next time. "When the going gets tough, the tough get going," Kennedy was fond of telling his children.

To help Joe, and in turn the other children, become racing champions, Kennedy hired an experienced adult skipper to be in charge of the boats and supervise the youngsters. The first skipper was a drinking man. One day, when Joe found him drinking beer, the skipper was so embarrassed he poured the beer into his paint can. "That will give the boat added buoyancy," he offered as a quick excuse. But he proved to be a good teacher. Joe and Jack began winning so regularly that the story spread they were cheating by using sails larger than regulation size. However, all boats were thoroughly inspected before races, and the Kennedy boats were always in order.

Joe never raced against Jack, yet their competition continued at Hyannis Port over boats. A friend of Joe recalled: "Usually they'd get into a hassle at home because Joe would want to take the boat one place and Jack would want to take it another. So they'd fight. Joe was bigger, and he'd win and take the boat. But then Jack would go along with him, just as happy as can be."

By 1929 Kennedy headed three large movie studios in Hollywood and served as special adviser to a fourth at a consultant's fee of $150,000 a year. Priding himself on being a shrewd businessman, he believed his ability applied to any type of business transaction. One time he bought a boat he considered an enormous bargain without consulting his skipper and Joe. On examination, the two found that the screws on the engine were completely rusty, a sign of years of total neglect. When the skipper advised him to junk the vessel as a dead loss, Kennedy sharply ordered him to put it into seaworthy condition. This turned out to be a matter of pouring good money after bad. Eventually the hopelessness of the task was revealed when the boat was lowered into the harbor and promptly sank.

By 1929 Kennedy was so wealthy that he established a $1,000,000-trust fund for each of his children. Two later trust funds promised each Kennedy $10,000,000 at the age of forty-five. However, the children were not told about their status as millionaires. The discussion of money was forbidden in the house, and their allowances were tiny.

## Joseph Patrick Kennedy, Jr.

No one in Hyannis Port would have guessed Joe and Jack belonged to a rich family. When they walked into town, they wore threadbare shorts and were barefooted. It was a common sight for fourteen-year-old millionaire Joe and twelve-year-old millionaire Jack to be arguing with the ticket seller at the Idlewood movie house that they were just big for their ages and should be admitted at the ten-cent price for children under twelve. The owner of the Rexall drugstore not only was displeased when they read his magazines without buying any but grew alarmed when they brought their fox terrier along. For the Kennedy dog would leap into the window to chase the cat sleeping in the warm sunlight. When the boys were old enough for driver's licenses, their father gave them so little money that they were able to buy only jalopies. Joe's car was a tan Ford roadster whose hood was kept in place with a heavy rope. Jack's car was equally an eyesore with loose, dented fenders and a radiator grill that was crushed.

Mr. Kennedy was able to take on the direct task of overseeing his children year round beginning in 1929. For that year he left the movie industry and sold his large holdings of stocks shortly before the market crash in October. He had time now to help mold Joe, who he believed would one day become an important American —perhaps even President of the United States.

After Joe finished at the Riverdale Country School, his father selected the Choate School at Wallingford, Connecticut, as the place for him to prepare for Harvard. Choate, established in 1896 as a boarding school for well-to-do youngsters, was top-rated academically. Dr. George

St. John, the headmaster, was a scholarly man, who believed in combining education with character building. He maintained intimate classes—a master for every ten students—and the faculty lived with the boys in the series of houses on the school grounds.

Joe did well in Latin, French, English, and history, but his specialties were outdoor sports and student leadership. He was a strong canoeist on the nearby Quinnipiac River, an excellent horseman, a swift runner, and a far-jumping skier. In group sports he was a never-pessimistic team player, who starred at end on the undefeated Choate football team of 1932.

The elder Kennedy was proud when Joe became editor of the yearbook. But his chest really swelled when Joe won the coveted Harvard Football Trophy before his graduation in the spring of 1933. This was a special award made annually "to that member of the Choate football squad who best combines scholarship and sportsmanship."

That summer, when Joe went to Hyannis Port, he did little sailing, for he was intent on doing well that fall in his courses as a Harvard freshman. Every morning he rose early to drive to the Bilmore Tutoring Studios in town, where he had enrolled as a special student for brushup work in several subjects. Such slavish use of his time during vacation months caught the attention of his father, who decided to reward Joe for his special effort.

In the news at that time was Professor Harold Laski, a brilliant teacher at the London School of Economics. Although British, Laski was a noted authority on the American Presidency, and his books and magazine articles were widely read in the United States. Laski's reputation as a teacher stemmed from the enthusiasm of his students, who said he had taught them to think logically. In philosophy, Laski was a Socialist, advocating government ownership of industry and property.

Joseph Kennedy's philosophy was the opposite of Laski's, for he was a firm believer in a free enterprise system. Yet he felt that Joe might benefit immensely by studying a year with Laski before starting Harvard. "Laski was a nut and a crank," said Kennedy. "I disagreed with everything he wrote. But I never taught the boys to disapprove of someone just because I didn't like him. They heard enough from me, and I decided they should be exposed to someone of intelligence and vitality on the other side."

Joe, accepting his father's offer enthusiastically, sailed to England when the school year began that fall. He found Professor Laski a thin man with a mustache and large round glasses, a man whose weak physical appearance was immediately forgotten when he began expressing the thoughts of his remarkable mind. Laski's classes at the London School were crowded with young people with high IQ's, and the give-and-take discussions between professor and students were considered a treat by outsiders.

The young American and Laski were friends from the start, and Joe found the professor's classes exciting. The school's curriculum required him to attend seven lectures a week and write a weekly essay on a philosophical subject. "His mind was only just beginning to discover the enchantment of thought," was the way Laski described Joe's ability to argue with more advanced students. But Laski considered it to be an excellent mind, and he ad-

43

mired Joe's "astounding vitality" and "profound interest in politics."

"He had his heart set on a political career," Laski later recalled. "He often sat in my study and submitted with that smile that was pure magic to relentless teasing about his determination to be nothing less than the President of the United States."

The London School of Economics was the first coeducational institution Joe had attended, and he was a favorite of the British girls in his classes. As a change of pace from serious studies, the London School frequently held dances to help the students relax. Laski, observing Joe at the dances, wrote: "I think that handsome boy made the heart of many a girl beat rather more quickly."

When the school year came to an end in the spring of 1934, Laski and his wife had grown so attached to Joe that they included him in their summer plans. This was a tour of the Soviet Union, which gave Joe the opportunity to observe the Communist dictatorship firsthand and begin Harvard that fall as a more mature freshman.

Members of college freshmen classes are often given to high jinks, and Harvard was no exception. However, Joe always refused to join in the pranks. One reason was that he was an "old" freshman at nineteen. Another was that he had just been through his broadening year with Laski.

Still another explanation was one he made to Timothy "Ted" J. Reardon, his closest friend at Harvard. "You know, T.J.," he once told Reardon, "I'm the oldest of my family, and I've got to be the example for a lot of brothers and sisters." Yet when the opportunity came to join a highly prized club on the campus, he swallowed his determination and suffered through a lowly initiation. Ordered to keep a large haddock strapped around his waist for a week, he did this, even though no one would come within several feet of him after the second day.

Many fellow students who lived with him in Winthrop House on the Harvard Yard, as the campus is called, treated him with awe. The principal reason was that he had come to college with a valet, genial George Taylor. It was Taylor's job to make life simpler for his young charge by taking care of his clothes, running errands, and acting as a father confessor. Once Joe caused friends to gulp by sending Taylor by airplane to New York to drive his jalopy back to Cambridge. Taylor also took indirect part in Joe's schoolwork by serving as his audience when Joe rehearsed classroom talks.

Despite seemingly endless outside activities, Joe consistently maintained good grades. One of Joe's secrets was that he planned his day in advance and tried to use every minute profitably. "I don't think I can remember seeing him sit back in a chair and relax," said Jack, who later followed his brother to Harvard. "Even when still there was always a sense of motion forcibly restrained. This continuous motion came from his intense enthusiasm for everything he did and his exceptional stamina."

Another of his secret weapons was that he tried constantly to improve himself. For instance, he came to college with a miserable handwriting. Every day he set time aside for writing practice; when the improvement was slight, he turned to printing. Finally, he bought a typewriter; when he had an unexpected few minutes between activities, he would rush to the machine and work on accuracy and speed.

This burning desire to improve himself also extended to football. Although he made the freshman team as a rangy, hard end with 185 pounds on his six-foot two-inch frame, every day following practice he had Ted Reardon throw passes to him for an additional hour. Even when the regular season ended after Thanksgiving, the two continued this practice each day until summer vacation.

Reardon and others also discovered Joe's unusual loyalty to his family. Joe always spoke reverently about Grampa Honey Fitz, calling him "the greatest mayor Boston ever had." One time, when Reardon in jest made a belittling remark about Honey Fitz, Joe's face turned red with rage, and he screamed at his best friend, "Get out of this room!" Reardon never said it again.

When the freshman year ended in June, 1935, Joe was already the best-known member of his class. A member of the football team and the student council, a good student, and a favorite of the girls, Joe had much joy as he set off for Hyannis Port with George Taylor in his jalopy. But some of his happiness vanished after he and Jack won a major sailing race and staged a victory party at the local hotel.

It was a pleasant party until several of the boys grew noisy. When they would not lower their voices, the management finally summoned the police. Apologies by the party givers failed to satisfy the officers, and Joe and Jack were taken to the local jail. There Joe was permitted the usual single phone call. Since his father was out of town, he called the skipper of the Kennedy boats. Joe's plea was that he come immediately to post bail so they would not have to spend the night in a cell.

However, the skipper was in a fierce mood, for he had been arguing with the Kennedy girls, who persisted in dropping their clothes and towels on the pier as they walked home with the expectation that he would pick up after them. In order to gain indirect revenge, the skipper told the jailer to keep the boys behind bars "to teach them a lesson." Not until morning were they released.

Back at Harvard in the fall, Joe returned once more to center stage among his fellow students. But again he had a run-in with the law, and again he was not at fault. Robert Downes, his roommate at Winthrop House, recalled one night that Joe walked in, shrugged, and said that he had been in jail. Joe explained that he had been walking a few blocks from Harvard Square when he suddenly heard a scream. He ran to investigate and found a man beating a woman in a parked car. Without hesitation, he yanked open the door and came to the defense of the woman. But when he pulled the man from the car, the woman began hitting Joe, and the noise of the enlarged battle soon brought a police wagon to the scene. The man and woman were able to outtalk Joe when the police asked for an explanation, with the result that they were allowed to walk away while he was carted to jail. Only after repeated explanation of the true events was he released.

Joe's undergraduate years at Harvard passed swiftly. His name was frequently in the Boston papers for his activities as a member of the Crimson football and rugby teams. Eddie Moore, who had been Honey Fitz's secretary and now worked for Joseph Kennedy, was Joe's self-appointed trumpeter, and he spoke of Joe's battle scars on the football field: ". . . a bad banging of a knee, an arm broken, a busted nose." Moore also spoke proudly of the young man when he went to Switzerland on vacation, and "although a complete novice, he came within two seconds of the world's record for the bobsled ride." That same winter, Moore recorded, Joe "suffered a gash in the elbow to the bone on a ski run down a mountainside."

Quiet Jack Kennedy, still living in his brother's shadow, had followed Joe to Harvard from Choate after a slight detour at Princeton. At Harvard, he had moved into Winthrop House, where Joe was student head. Every night the two had dinner together, and occasionally they went to a movie or a Boston tryout of a musical comedy heading for Broadway. But each had his own friends and led a separate existence. Yet their dominant interest in their family remained an unbreakable bond between them. Mrs. George de Pinto, in charge of the dining room, saw the depth of the bond one night in 1938, when Joseph Kennedy came to Winthrop House as a dinner speaker. She was thrilled when the two young men rushed to the head table and kissed their father in front of the large crowd.

Both boys were also united by their interest in sailing. In Joe's last year, they formed the Crimsons' undefeated two-man team. They stirred great excitement at the intercollegiate race when theirs was the first boat across the finish line and they won the treasured MacMillan Cup. That the two Kennedy boys had far different personalities was evident at the banquet that evening in their honor. "Jack looked like a nice enough kid, but it was Joe you noticed and remembered," said one man. "He

*Joseph Patrick Kennedy, Jr.*

had a very magnetic personality. He seemed to know everybody at the banquet and everybody seemed to know him."

In his senior year, Joe was chairman of the student council and his class day committee, financial manager of the yearbook, and chairman of the smoker committee. In addition, he was graduated with honors in international relations. Dr. Payson Wild, his faculty adviser, called him a young man who "bubbled over with energy, ideas and fun" and possessed "charm, humor and good sense." His roommate reported that classmates had asked, "How does one guy do so many things so well?" Others wanted to know how he managed to have so many beautiful girlfriends. "You'd always see Joe in his convertible, the top down, and the prettiest girl in town beside him," said one observer.

When graduation day came in June, 1938, there was no doubt among Joe's classmates that he would be a vital public figure one day. His brother Jack said: "Of all the people I have ever met, Joe had truly the mark of greatness on him." After the cap and gown ceremonies, Joe asked his friends to wait while he looked for Mrs. de Pinto. He handed her a package containing a gardenia for each of his years at Winthrop House, and half in jest he told her, "Deedee, you shouldn't have to work here. When I become President, I'll take you to the White House with me."

During the four years that Joe spent at Harvard, his father had been an extremely busy man. In 1932 Joseph Kennedy had campaigned actively for Franklin Delano Roosevelt. He had gone along as an adviser on his cross-country campaign train and contributed money to help

49

pay campaign expenses. Afterward he told Joe he expected to be named as Roosevelt's Secretary of the Treasury. But the best job offered him was that of chairman of the Securities and Exchange Commission, which had the task of regulating stock market operations. The elder Kennedy accepted this job in 1934, rented a twenty-five-room house in Rockville, Maryland, 10 miles from Washington, and commuted weekends to his family in Bronxville and Hyannis Port. Once when Joe and Jack came to visit him, he took them to the White House to meet Roosevelt.

After a year as chairman of the SEC, where he earned a reputation as a first-class administrator, Kennedy resigned and received a $200,000 fee from RCA for drawing up a recapitalization plan. From Paramount Pictures, he received $55,000 for drawing up a plan to reorganize the company. He also became a $10,000-a-week consultant to the Hearst newspaper empire. In addition, he gained an exclusive franchise to sell popular British liquors in the United States.

Having had a taste of public life, however, Mr. Kennedy sought further jobs from the Roosevelt Administration. In 1936 he wrote a book, *I'm for Roosevelt,* and after the President's sweeping victory for a second term, he brought Kennedy back into the government. This time he named him head of the Federal Maritime Commission, with the task of creating a large and busy American merchant fleet. Then, early in 1938, Roosevelt gave him the nation's most important diplomatic post, appointing him Ambassador to Great Britain.

Originally, it was Joe's intention to enroll in Harvard

Law School in the fall of 1938. But with the European continent in growing turmoil because of Adolf Hitler's aggressions, Joe decided to spend a year in Europe to view events in person.

His European venture began with a sentimental trip to Ireland with his father. The formal excuse for their journey was to go to Dublin, where the National University was to award the ambassador an honorary degree. But their chief destination was a mud-floor, windowless, thatched-roof cottage in County Wexford. There Pat Kennedy had slept on the ground and warmed his potatoes in the peat fire until that day ninety years previously, when he had left for America.

After their view of the humble origins of the Kennedy clan, Joe worked for his father briefly in the elegant thirty-six-room U.S. embassy in London. Then, at Joe's request, his father asked U.S. Ambassador to France, William C. Bullitt, to hire him as one of his secretaries.

That September British Prime Minister Neville Chamberlain and French Premier Édouard Daladier made an anxious trip to Munich, Germany, where they gave Hitler part of Czechoslovakia in the mistaken belief that this would satisfy him and prevent World War II. While the Munich crisis was boiling, Ambassador Bullitt sent Joe with secret dispatches to the American Embassy in the Czech capital of Prague, where the young man was a witness to history as it developed. Bullitt also sent him to Warsaw, Leningrad, Stockholm, Copenhagen, and the Nazi capital at Berlin. In the non-Germanic countries Joe observed the fears of the people, while in Berlin he saw the eagerness of would-be aggressors with their modern tanks and planes.

## The Kennedy Brothers

In July, 1936, civil war had broken out in Spain, where an army colonel named Francisco Franco undertook a successful three-year fight to overthrow the republican government and establish a dictatorship. The war was not confined to Spaniards, for Germany and Italy came to the aid of Franco's Insurgents with men and equipment, while the Soviet Union did the same for the government Loyalists. The United States maintained its neutrality.

After three months with Ambassador Bullitt, Joe wanted to go to Spain for a long look at the Civil War, which was being won by Franco at a cost of hundreds of thousands of civilian and military casualties. Despite the opposition of his father, who did not want his son to enter this dangerous area, Joe armed himself with passports and left for Spain. When he landed at Valencia on the east coast, he cabled his father: SORRY I MISSED YOU. ARRIVED SAFELY IN VALENCIA. GOING MADRID TONIHGT. Valencia, on the Mediterranean, was then only one of nine provincial capitals remaining in the hands of the Loyalist government; Franco had already captured the other forty-three.

The devastated country between Valencia and Madrid, the national capital, some 300 miles inland, was controlled in some areas by the Franco Insurgents and in other places by the Loyalists. For safe-conduct through the lines, Joe had passports to both warring sides, but this only made each suspicious that he might really be a spy for the other belligerent. In one town controlled by the Insurgents, he was immediately imprisoned when he showed his Loyalist passport by mistake. An Amer-

52

ican newsman on the scene reported: "He [Joe, Jr.] was released only after his clothes were taken off and lemon juice rubbed on his epidermis to see whether invisible ink messages were written thereon."

Joe spent seven weeks in Madrid, then under heavy air pounding and siege by the Franco Insurgents. When he arrived in this city of 1,200,000 persons, the New York *Herald Tribune* ran a news story on February 16, 1939, with the heading: JUST IN TIME FOR DAILY SHELL-ING. The story was about Joe and quoted him as saying he had come to Madrid to "see for himself what it was like to live in a besieged city on a diet of sardines and rice."

Kathleen (Kick) came to Madrid from London for a short visit with her brother, and she worried about him when she learned that he walked through the city without fear as bullets ripped into buildings all about him. One time, she said, he was caught in a heavy crossfire and had to dive under a truck to avoid the bullets. To take Kick's mind off the war, Joe invited her to go swimming one day. Despite the horrors of three years of war, prudish Spanish customs had been retained. When Joe approached the water wearing swim trunks, the other swimmers gasped at him. Police quickly surrounded him, scolded him for a lack of decency, and ordered him to put on a shirt.

Joe was in Madrid when it fell to Franco on March 28, 1939, and he watched helplessly as Loyalist friends were dragged off to prison. During Madrid's last days he wrote frequently to his father, detailing events in the Spanish capital. The letters were so informative and interesting, said his father, that British Prime Minister Chamberlain requested permission to read them.

After Spain, Joe returned to England, where he worked as his father's private secretary until it was time to go home to begin law school. Hitler had seized the rest of Czechoslovakia in March; then, when Germany and the Communist Soviet Union signed a military alliance in May, World War II drew close. It began on September 1, when Germany invaded Poland. Two days later England and France declared war on Germany.

Fearing that the British Isles would soon be bombed by Hitler's air force, the 9,000 Americans in England flooded the U.S. Embassy in London with requests for aid to return home. Ambassador Kennedy turned this assignment over to Joe, who efficiently gathered a list of tramp steamers then in English ports. With this master list and the cooperation of ship officials, he calmed worried Americans by arranging passage back to the United States for them.

In an ocean now plagued with German submarines, he sailed for home after finishing his job and returned to Cambridge to begin his three-year course of study at Harvard Law School. He tried at first to act the part of the older college man by transferring his valet, George Taylor, to his brother Jack and moving into the Bay State Apartments for a more adult atmosphere. But Mrs. Alice Harrington, who owned the apartment house, said he never lost his undergraduate enthusiasm. "I remember the many times Joe would assemble twenty-five or more in front of the house and with banners and placards, he, seated on the hood of his car," she said, "led them down Massachusetts Avenue toward Harvard

*Joseph Patrick Kennedy, Jr.*

Square—where to and what for I never knew." She also saw him frequently as he returned from classes with his green book bag thrown over a shoulder and with half a dozen or more young men surrounding him, "all arguing and gesticulating. He was like a magnet and when he left, they disbanded." It turned out later that the placards and the talk dealt with domestic and international politics.

In early 1940 Joe made his first political campaign. The Democratic National Convention was to nominate a Presidential candidate in Chicago that summer, and he thought it an excellent way to begin his political career by winning a seat in the Massachusetts delegation. There was as yet no indication from President Roosevelt that he planned to run for a third term, with the result that several Democrats were publicized as candidates for the nomination. One was Joseph Kennedy, who received early newspaper boosts before others gained far greater attention.

The district Joe hoped to represent was the slum area of Boston's West End, where Grampa Honey Fitz was still considered to be popular. But Joe took nothing for granted and spent valuable time away from law classes to knock on every door in the district and ask for support. Joe was on a delegation ticket pledged to vote at the convention for Postmaster General James Farley, and when Farley won the state's primary contest, Joe became a delegate.

Between the primary and the July 15 national convention, President Roosevelt was cautiously edging his way toward admitting he might not be opposed to breaking the two-term tradition for American Presidents. By

55

the time the forty-eight state delegations were in their seats, few doubted that he would be a candidate once more, and a stampede developed in most delegations to change their votes, already committed to other candidates, to the support of Roosevelt.

Massachusetts was no exception. William "Onions" Burke, chairman of the Massachusetts delegation, was eager to swing his state behind the President. But when he polled the delegation to win its consent to switch from Farley to Roosevelt, Joe refused to change his vote.

This led Democratic Party leaders to place a frantic call to Ambassador Kennedy in London to urge him to "talk some sense into his boy." But Kennedy refused to exert the slightest influence on Joe. "No, I wouldn't think of telling my son what to do," he told his callers.

Roosevelt easily won renomination on the first ballot, but he failed to get the unanimous vote he had sought. "I remember that resolute young voice [of Joe Kennedy] calling 'James A. Farley' when the Massachusetts delegation was polled," said Farley afterward.

Yet even though he had held out to the bitter end against the President's nomination, Joe worked for Roosevelt's election that fall. When the President came to Boston on his campaign tour of New England, Joe, Jack, and Grampa Honey Fitz went to the South Station yard to visit him aboard his train. "As we entered," Jack recalled, "Franklin Delano Roosevelt threw his arms out and said to Grampa, 'Welcome Dulce Adeline [Sweet Adeline].' He explained that when he visited South America in the late 1930's, he had been surprised to hear a band that was supposed to play the national anthem break into the strains of 'Sweet Adeline.' 'They told me that some years ago,' the President continued, 'a distinguished Bostonian traveled through their country singing 'Dulce Adeline' at every stop until finally the people were convinced the song must be America's national anthem.' "

Like all young American men, Joe registered for the draft in October, 1940. In Europe, Hitler's forces had overrun the Continent and had captured Norway, Denmark, Holland, Belgium, and France. By midyear his air force was bombing England around the clock in what became known as the Battle of Britain. Meanwhile, in Asia, Hitler's ally Japan had captured Manchuria and moved southward through China and French Indochina.

Oddly, Hitler's numerous successes on the battlefield weakened Ambassador Kennedy's standing as a diplomat. He had started as an extremely popular envoy when he first came to London in the spring of 1938. Crowds gathered to see the "nine-child envoy" and newspapers heaped much attention on the Kennedy family and its doings. Part of an ambassador's job was to strive to become a friend of the government's leader, and Kennedy had quickly succeeded in establishing warm relations with British Prime Minister Chamberlain. Unfortunately, after Chamberlain gave part of free Czechoslovakia to Hitler at Munich, the Prime Minister's popularity with his people declined. Then, when Kennedy began making speeches and press statements justifying Chamberlain's policy, his own popularity declined as well.

It was Kennedy's view that in a war between Britain and Germany, the well-prepared Nazis would win. He favored strict American neutrality in the struggle between those nations because he believed American aid to

Britain with supplies and arms would make no difference in the outcome. As for direct American intervention on the battlefield, he strongly opposed this. "I have four boys," he told a friend, "and I don't want them to be killed in a foreign war."

President Roosevelt's views, in sharp contrast with those of his ambassador, held that England's survival was essential to the free world, and he believed American aid would prevent her defeat by Germany. As a result, he proceeded to supply England with naval vessels, arms, and equipment. This put Kennedy in the position of being opposed to his boss, and he resigned as ambassador shortly after the 1940 election.

A great debate had begun to rage across the United States between isolationists and interventionists at about the time Joseph Kennedy returned, and he joined the forces of the isolationists as a leader. Young Joe Kennedy, always proud of his father, agreed with his position. While in his second year in law school, he traveled throughout Massachusetts to deliver speeches opposing American intervention in the war. He also debated Harvard professors on the issue, although he pointed out that he was not a pacifist and favored strengthening America's military might quickly.

The more he advocated a larger Army and Navy, the more Joe felt it a sham that he remain a civilian. In June, 1941, he completed his second year in law school; only one year remained before he got his degree. On July 10 he sailed his boat in the big eight-mile race off Nantucket Sound. Those who talked to him before the race said that his mind did not seem to be on the event.

And for good reason. The following day he reported

to Squantum Island Naval Air Station outside Boston for basic training leading to a commission as a Navy pilot. With his father's connections, he could easily have won appointment to the staff of a desk admiral in Washington. But he refused to consider this.

When reporters came to Squantum to ask why he had joined the service after opposing the convoying of supplies to England, Joe replied, "My ideas haven't changed. I still don't think we should go into the war. But I thought I ought to do something, and I'll do whatever they tell me to do. My father, especially, approves of what I am doing."

Again reporters came to Squantum to interview him, and this time Joe grew angry. "There are seventy-nine of us here," he said. "And I don't want more attention than you give them."

After thirty days as a seaman second class at Squantum, Joe was sent to the naval station at Jacksonville, Florida, for his flight training. Captain Maurice Sheehy, chaplain there, remembered long afterward the tall young man "with sturdy football shoulders, whose hair as well as his face appeared sunburned." There was a month's delay before he could be sworn in as a cadet, and Joe asked if he could help out during that time by working on the station's publicity.

Within a few days all those employed in the business office were asking Joe for advice about their jobs. "Is this kid stretching to be CO [commanding officer] of the station?" an officer asked Sheehy.

When Joe began his training as an aviation cadet, said Father Sheehy, he realized that more was expected from him than from the other men because of his father's prominence. A cadet's day began at 5:45 A.M. and continued until 10 P.M. There were numerous classes, piles of homework, hours of training in the skies. Beyond that the cadets were held accountable for their quarters. Station officers were constantly concerned that they would be accused of being kind to Joe because his father had been an ambassador and a man close to the President. So they were twice as strict as necessary with Joe. He realized that he had to make his room gleam in perfect cleanliness, for a dust particle found anywhere would result in extra rifle drill after an exhausting day.

On his few days off, Joe relaxed by playing golf with Sheehy, and generally they made small bets on each hole. On one occasion, when Sheehy could not play in a foursome, he told Joe to keep the date by pitting himself against the other two. Sheehy was a prankster. Instead of warning Joe that his opponents were excellent golfers, he said they were duffers. He advised him to give each a one-stroke handicap on every hole and bet heavily on the outcome.

On the first hole, when his two opponents played with the skill of top professionals, Joe told himself it was an accident. But when they won the second hole just as easily, he bit his lip and cursed aloud, "I've been framed by a chaplain!"

Pearl Harbor plunged the United States into sudden war with Japan on December 7, 1941. A few days later, when Germany and Italy declared war on the United States, World War II became a global conflict. There were now no isolationists or interventionists. The country was involved in a life or death struggle.

60

## Joseph Patrick Kennedy, Jr.

When Joe's class was graduated in May, 1942, his father was invited to be guest speaker. The elder Kennedy beamed on learning that Joe's fellow ensigns had elected him to receive the gold Cutler Wings, awarded to "that cadet best fitted for his duties as a U.S. Naval Officer." At the station, he had also served as president of the Cadet Club and the Holy Name Society, and after Mr. Kennedy pinned the gold wings on his son's jacket, Sheehy confided to the father that Joe had put the Cadet Club "on such a sound financial basis that its assets became a problem."

After graduation, Joe had hopes of being assigned to a forward base in England. Therefore, he was disappointed when the Navy sent him on antisubmarine patrol duty in the Caribbean area. There was action there, however, for German submarines prowled the routes of the numerous merchant ship convoys. Joe would not discuss his experiences on this duty, though Father Sheehy learned that in one fight "he nearly lost his plane and himself."

Upon completing a year of Caribbean duty, Joe was advanced to full lieutenant and transferred to England. He was to fly with the newly organized U.S. Fairwing Seven Squadron, which would be attached to the Royal Air Force (RAF) Coastal Command, a highly active fighting force.

In August, 1943, he came home to Hyannis Port for a last holiday before flying his big Liberator bomber across the Atlantic. He seemed much older to his family and friends. On Joe's twenty-first birthday his father had given him $1,000 because he had not smoked or tasted hard liquor. But now, at twenty-eight, Joe came home a smoker of long, black cigars.

Joe said little as he sailed the *Victura,* and he had few comments when Grampa Honey Fitz told the story of his unsuccessful try for the U.S. Senate the previous year. But just when Joe's relatives grew worried because his manner was so unnaturally quiet, he pulled a prank. There was a tiny naval station at the local airport, and Joe talked the personnel there into letting him borrow a plane. Minutes later he buzzed the large crowd along Hyannis Harbor. Outraged citizens phoned the Hyannis Airport, and through radio pleas Joe was "persuaded" to land and end his escapade.

There was little time for humor and pranks in bomb-torn England. When Joe's B-24 roared down the landing strip onto British soil, he found the people grim, their clothing shabby, but their determination high. For his sister Kick, now in England as a Red Cross worker, he had flown six dozen eggs across the Atlantic. Eggs were then extremely rare in the British Isles. One of Joe's crewmen delivered the eggs to Kick, and he told her about her brother's concern for the safety of the special cargo: "I certainly hope you enjoy those eggs," he said. "There wasn't anything Mr. Kennedy didn't make our plane do, on the excuse that those eggs should arrive fresh and unbroken."

The routine of the squadron to which Joe was attached was harsh. At the American station, he lived with other officers in corrugated iron huts. They flew by night and slept during the day. After dinner in the mess, they went by Jeep to the operations building for a briefing on the next patrol. Then they climbed into trucks for the ride to the field and their B-24's. There, after adjusting electrically heated leather flying suits and life jackets, they piled into their bombers for a midnight takeoff. Then they roared off on the usual 2,000-mile mission, with twelve hours of patrol duty.

Their flights took them over the Bay of Biscay, where they hunted for German submarines preying on Allied shipping. Toward noon, the surviving planes landed back at the station. The men climbed back into the trucks for the ride to Intelligence headquarters, where they were questioned on their activities and observations.

Kick said that Joe phoned her two or three times a week. When he came to London on leave, he saw her every day. Kick had a special problem at this time, and Joe acted the part of the substitute father he had been in her early years. She had fallen in love with William John Robert Cavendish, the young Marquess of Harting-ton, who was an officer in the Coldstream Guards.

She and Billy had become engaged, but marriage seemed out of the question because her parents opposed her marrying a non-Catholic. In addition, Billy's parents, the Duke and Duchess of Devonshire, did not want their son to marry a Catholic. Joe's advice was that she follow her heart and ignore both sets of parents. "Never did anyone have such a pillar of strength as I had in Joe in those difficult days before my marriage," said Kathleen.

Only at the last minute did Billy's parents agree to attend the civil wedding ceremony in May, 1944, and Kathleen was disappointed when her parents did not wire best wishes. But Joe was there to give his sister away, and his warm smile stood out in the wedding picture in contrast with the sad faces of the Duke and Duchess.

A month later, Billy Hartington was shipped to the coast with all leave canceled. Not long after that, Kick learned he had been killed in action in the costly Normandy campaign.

Casualties were also high in Joe's Navy patrol squadron. The planes flew in darkness and wretched weather. Accidents were commonplace. Frequently, groups of German night fighter planes, using a U-boat as a decoy, attacked and shot down the big Liberator bombers. Nevertheless, Joe and his crew came through their flights unharmed.

In May, 1944, they had completed their required num ber of missions and were being processed for return to the United States. But Joe had learned about the coming Normandy invasion with a June D Day landing, and he persuaded his men to stay on in order to take part in the D Day assault.

During the hectic opening period of the invasion of the European continent across the English Channel, Joe's crew swiftly completed a full second tour of duty. This time, when it was over, Joe insisted they go home and not test their luck further.

Joe's gear pack was already aboard a ship when he heard about an unusual mission that lacked trained pilots. Further investigation revealed that the mission would probably be suicidal for crews, but he figured out that for someone trained as he was, survival odds were closer to a 50–50 chance. "I don't mind those odds," he told a friend.

Officers in charge of the mission tried to discourage Joe. He had done more than his duty already, they told him. Besides, he was war-weary. But he waved aside their arguments and insisted on signing on as a participant. Training took place at a special base at Fersfield, in southern England. The purpose was to knock out heavily fortified German V-1 sites along the North Sea. These pilotless missiles had struck first in London on June 16, ten days after D Day, and General Dwight D. Eisenhower later admitted that had they fallen before the invasion, there would have been no D Day. Within weeks, London was turning into a city of bomb craters, and casualties were frightening.

At Fersfield the plan of attack was based on the assumption that regular planes could not survive the ground-to-air explosives circling the V-1 launching sites. So the scheme called for loading the bomb bay of a B-24 Liberator with 10 tons of Torpex (a combination of TNT, dynamite, aluminum powder, and wax). A television camera was set in the nose of the four-engine bomber, and the pilot turned it on when he took off from the air strip. Once in the air, he was to head directly toward the V-1 site, and the continuous pictures from his TV camera would appear on the screen of a "mother" airplane 20 miles behind him.

When the mother plane told him he was on course, he was to pull a switch that placed the bomber on remote control. Next, he would pull another switch that set the fuses to go off on schedule. After this, he and his co-pilot were to bail out over the sea and leave the job of guiding their bomber drone to the mother plane. Rendezvousing ships were to pick up the pilots once they hit the water.

Joe celebrated his twenty-ninth birthday at Fersfield on July 25, 1944. One week later, on August 2, he watched his Liberator being loaded with Torpex. His was to be a special mission that day. Instead of heading for a V-1 site, he was to nose his plane toward the well-guarded Nazi submarine base on Helgoland, a German island in the North Sea.

Joe took off with Lieutenant Wilford Willy from Fort Worth, Texas, as his copilot. Both had received intensive special training and were well prepared for the daring mission. Minutes after their smooth takeoff, they were flying over the English Channel on their way to the target.

Next came notification to the mother plane that they had switched the plane to remote control. All that remained was to pull the switch on the ammunition fuses before the bailout.

But they never got out. The mother plane reported that the sky suddenly turned bright orange as two massive explosions tore the Liberator to pieces. Along with Willy's, Joe Kennedy's short life had ended.

Back at the base, Ensign James Simpson was grief-stricken. "I was in the plane testing and double checking with Joe before take off, and I said, 'So long, and good luck, Joe. I only wish I were going with you.' He answered, 'Thanks, Jim. Don't forget, you're going to make the next one with me. . . . Say, by the way, if I don't come back, you fellows can have the rest of my eggs.' "

Not long after the explosions, two priests came to the Kennedy home at Hyannis Port to see Joseph Kennedy. They broke the news of his son's death to him in private and then left. When they were gone, he stumbled from the room, his face moist with tears, to tell his wife and children the terrible news. After this, he walked to his room and locked the door behind him.

Years later, the mere mention of his son's name moved him to tears.

# 3 John Fitzgerald Kennedy

ONLY after his older brother died in the skies over the English Channel did John F. Kennedy emerge from Joe's shadow. In the sad months that followed, whenever problems arose, he found himself saying, "If Joe were here, he'd do it this way . . . ." But in time, while the ache over losing his brother remained, his own personality began to flower, and he started the brilliant political career that was to carry him to the Presidency and world leadership.

There were advantages and disadvantages for John F. Kennedy in growing up as a member of the Joseph P. Kennedy household. There was the lively political background that came from being a grandson of two Irish politicians who operated in Boston—Patrick Joseph Kennedy and John Francis "Honey Fitz" Fitzgerald.

There was also the wealth of his father and with this the plush ease of the rich—homes in the suburbs and alongside the ocean, a villa on the French Riviera, servants, private schools, travel abroad, and large sailboats.

Chiefly by holding their children to tiny allowances did the Kennedy parents hope to keep them from becoming spoiled. On the occasion when he became a Boy Scout, Jack, who was an extremely poor speller, voiced objection to his "poverty." In a letter to his father, he complained: "My recent allowance is 40¢. This I use for areoplanes and other playthings of childhood, but now I am a scout and I put away my childish things. Before I would spend 20¢ of my 40¢ and In five minutes I would have empty pockets and nothing to gain and 20¢ to lose. When I am a scout I have to buy canteens, haversacks, blankets, searchliegs poncho things that will last for years and I can always use it while I can't use cholcolote marshmellow sunday with ice cream and so I put in my plea for a raise of thirty cents for me to buy schut things and pay my own way more around."

Even though the advantages of the Kennedy household were enormous, it held some drawbacks for Jack. There was no privacy in a family of nine children, and shy, sensitive Jack required some solitude. In addition, the driving father kept repeating that all his children must win at whatever they undertook. Furthermore, the father had focused his family ambitions on his son Joe's future.

Because of his father's demand that he must excel, throughout most of his childhood and youth, Jack remained a disappointment to Joseph Kennedy. Outside of sailing and a love of history and biography, he would not apply himself to other activities. "Now, Jack, I don't want to give the impression that I am a nagger, for goodness knows that is the worst thing a parent can be," the elder Kennedy wearily wrote his teen-age son. "After long experience in sizing up people I definitely know you have the goods and can go a long way. Now aren't you foolish not to get all there is out of what God has given you? It is very difficult to make up fundamentals that you have neglected when you were very young and that is why I am always urging you to do the best you can."

When Jack was born in Brookline, Massachusetts, on May 29, 1917, his brother Joe was almost two years old. Usually, in early years, an older brother bears a natural antagonism toward a younger brother because he senses that his special position in the family no longer exists. In the case of the Kennedy boys this was not so, for it was apparent to all that Joe held a unique place in the family.

Instead, it was Jack who maintained a continuing rivalry with Joe, and the relentless frustration of losing every fight and contest against his stronger brother put a damper on his childhood years. This losing competition brought on a desire to attend schools where Joe was not enrolled. It also gave rise to his extreme untidiness and poor schoolwork, in an effort to gain his father's attention.

Jack started his education at the Dexter Academy, a private school in Brookline, a year after Joe began. Then he transferred with Joe to the Riverdale Country School in the West Bronx when his father moved the family to New York in 1926. Jack's first attempt at independence came in 1930, when he finished Riverdale. Joe had gone on to Choate, the exclusive school in Wallingford, Connecticut, where he was immediately a star athlete and much admired youth. Joseph Kennedy, faced with a barrage of pleas by Jack against being sent to Choate, finally relented and allowed him to go to Canterbury, a prep school for rich Catholic boys in New Milford, Connecticut. This was a major concession on the part of the elder Kennedy, for he had vowed to send his sons to non-Catholic schools.

"I will be quite pius," wrote poor-spelling Jack to his religious mother that fall after his arrival at Canterbury. He also let his father know he was taking part in "football pracite" and was learning "baggamon," and he asked him to "please send me the Litary Digest because I did not know about the Market Slump until a long time after."

Not long afterward, an excited Jack wrote again to his father about his effort to become a football star like Joe. In practice, he said, "one fellow was running for a touchdown. I made a flying tackle and landed him. One of there fellow was seventeen and when he hit you you stayed hit. One time I got him out and what a pleasure it was to see him roll and writher on the ground."

But he failed to make the football squad because he was so spindly. He also became a concern to his mother because he lost so many gloves, socks, shoes, and books, and he annoyed his teachers, for he seemed bright, yet did so poorly in examinations. Although he boasted of getting a 98 in a test on *Ivanhoe,* his Latin teacher noted after a failing grade: "He can do better than this."

In the spring, Jack went home to New York for the

Easter holiday. A sharp attack of appendicitis prevented him from returning to school on time. Then he came down with diphtheria, and doctors feared he might die. By the fall his father had time to reconsider his approval of Canterbury, and he ruled that Jack would not return there. Instead, he sent him to Choate in the autumn of 1931 to be with Joe.

Again the sharp contrast between his two oldest sons came into clear focus. Joe was well on his way to winning the Harvard Football Trophy at Choate for the best combination of athletic and academic abilities, while Jack emerged as the winner of a pie-eating contest and as cheerleader. Jack's housemaster wrote his father: "Jack studies at the last minute, keeps appointments late, has little sense of material values, and can seldom locate his possessions."

Jack's letters home were filled with excuses and promises to do better. "If it were not for Latin I would probably lead the lower school," he told his mother. "But I am flunking that by ten points." He wrote again: "Maybe Dad thinks I am alibing but I am not. I have also been doing a little worrying about my studies because what he said about me starting of[f] great and then going down sunk in." Yet later he wrote his father: "I really feel now that I think it over that I have been bluffing myself about how much real work I have been doing."

To encourage Jack to study, his father gave him valuable presents for decent grades. These included a horse, a sailboat, and a trip to Europe, but the grades always fell down afterward. No presents by his father made him straighten out the room he shared with LeMoyne Billings at Choate. The disorder there was just a continuation of his existence at the Kennedy summer home at Hyannis Port, Massachusetts. Every summer, servants spoke to his mother in anger about the high pile of wet towels on his bedroom floor, the socks and ties that lay in a jumble in corners, and his overturned bureau drawers with their contents strewn on his bed.

A temporary change came over Jack in the fall of 1933, when he returned to Choate for his junior year. Joe was no longer there, and Jack's personality grew less shy and his grades improved. He began to feel less like a boy and more like a man and found himself popular with girls for the first time. He was described as being "tall, slender, wiry, with a small open face, snub nose and hair that bleached in the sun and resisted combing." "Jack was a very naughty boy when he was home," his youngest sister, Jean, confided to her father in a letter. "He kissed Betty Young under the mistletoe down in the front hall. He had a temperature of 102° one night, too, and Miss Cahill couldn't make him mind."

This growing sense of independence continued into Jack's senior year. His grades rose to the point where he managed to graduate sixty-fourth in a class of 112, or slightly below the center of the class of 1935. But far more significant was the personal assessment of his classmates, who elected him "the most likely to succeed."

Since Joe had delayed his registration at Harvard in order to spend a year with Professor Harold Laski at the London School of Economics, his father decided that Jack should have a similar experience. So, in the summer of 1935, following his graduation from Choate, Jack went to London. However, he had attended only a few classes of the Socialist professor when he came down with a severe case of jaundice. This forced him to drop out of school and come home to Hyannis Port to recuperate.

By the time the yellow tone of his skin and eyes was gone, American colleges had already begun the school year. Nevertheless, Jack did not want to waste the year, though he did not want to go to Harvard, where he would be subjected again to direct comparison with Joe, who was now a sophomore. With his father's permission, he enrolled at Princeton on October 12, 1935, and he moved into a dormitory with Lem Billings, his Choate roommate. But shortly before Christmas, his jaundice returned, and he was forced to drop out of Princeton. This time his father decreed that he must go to Arizona for a long rest and then follow Joe into Harvard in the fall of 1936.

Once more the rivalry with Joe resumed and, with it, the monotonous pattern of failure. Joe was on the Harvard football and rugby teams and an elected member of the student council. Jack's first order of business, therefore, was to win recognition as an athlete. He went out for football, swimming, and golf, and like Joe, he induced an outstanding football player to throw passes to him after practice. But though he stood six feet in height, he weighed only 149 pounds and he failed to make the regular Crimson squad. Swallowing his pride, he turned to the junior varsity, where his determination made up for his lack of weight. However, his football days ended on a short play when he was painfully injured, suffering a ruptured disk in his spine. This back injury was to prove almost fatal at a future time and caused physical agony for weeks and months at a time.

The Harvard swimming coach remembered Jack as "a

fine kid, frail and not too strong, but always giving it everything he had." This trait was borne out one time before the vital meet with Yale when the coach held races among his own squad members to determine who would represent Harvard. Jack hoped to swim the backstroke, but shortly before the Harvard team trials he fell ill with the flu and was put to bed in the Harvard infirmary. Even then he did not give up but had his roommate at Winthrop House bring steaks and malted milks to his hospital room in an effort to keep his weight from dropping. In addition, he climbed out of bed each day, dressed, and tiptoed out of the infirmary for a practice swim despite his high fever. But all his efforts came to naught, for in the trial race he failed to win the backstroke berth.

His lack of success in winning honors like Joe's extended beyond athletics. He was dismally swamped when he ran for president of the freshman class, and as a sophomore he did not win a post on the student council. Nor were his grades on a par with his brother. His father found time for a harsh lecture at the end of Jack's freshman year when his grades were all C's except for a single B. In his sophomore year, he maintained a C average only by getting a B in one course that offset a D in another.

During the 1930's almost all American college campuses were alive with student organizations arguing and protesting a variety of social, economic, and military issues. Harvard was no exception, and civil rights, the continuing depression, and the activities of dictators Hitler, Stalin, Mussolini, and Tojo were some of the emotional subjects aired. Jack Kennedy remained apart by not participating in the meetings and marches that took place. He wrote an occasional nonpolitical editorial for the *Harvard Crimson,* but beyond this his interests at Harvard were those of a rich young man whose existence seemed to center on becoming a member of the top social clubs in the Harvard Yard.

Not until he made a trip through Europe with Lem Billings in the summer of 1937 did he show a broadening of his interests. Among his stops on this two-month tour was one at the Vatican for an audience with his father's friend, Eugenio Cardinal Pacelli, who later became Pope Pius XII. Other than this meeting with an important person, Jack and Lem spent their time talking to reporters, people in the streets and in hotel lobbies in Italy, war-torn Spain, and France. In his diary Jack expressed his opinion that Fascism was popular in Italy and that "perhaps it would be better for Spain if Franco should win" even though the Spanish government "was in the right morally speaking." In a big generalization, he declared that "Fa[s]cism is the thing for Germany and Italy, Communism for Russia and Democracy for America and England." For a change of pace, he also went to a bullfight (which he considered a sickening spectacle of "cruelty"), climbed Mount Vesuvius in southern Italy, and won $1.20 at the gambling casino at Monte Carlo.

Jack's newfound interest in politics was revealed on his return to Harvard, where he decided to major in government. But his study habits were still so poor that a year passed before his grades began improving. By the time he started his junior year in September, 1938, his father was in London as the American ambassador. The elder Kennedy considered the timing perfect for Jack to discover if he had a calling for the diplomatic service as a career. For this reason, Jack talked the Harvard authorities into permitting him to spend the second semester probing the political situation throughout Europe. Early in 1939 he went to London, where he observed the hectic activities of his father to prevent the coming of World War II. But the elder Kennedy's support of Prime Minister Chamberlain's policy in behalf of peace was considered as a sign of British and American weakness by Hitler. As his father had done earlier for Joe, he arranged a job for Jack as a secretary to American Ambassador William Bullitt in Paris.

Jack spent six weeks with Bullitt in the spring of 1939. He learned that Bullitt's view of the tense international situation was the opposite of his father's. Bullitt's position was that the Munich Pact between Hitler's Germany and England and France was appeasement of the Nazi dictator and not a guaranty of European peace. By giving Hitler part of Czechoslavakia, Bullitt argued, the democratic leaders had only increased his appetite for more territory. The rest of Czechoslovakia, the free city of Danzig on the Baltic, and Poland were now in danger.

Before he went to Paris, Jack had agreed to act as his father's personal observer in France, Germany, Poland, the Baltic area, the Soviet Union, and the Middle East. As a special aid to Jack, the elder Kennedy had arranged to have him stay in the various American embassies in his travels.

After Paris, Jack went for three weeks to Poland, where he set up headquarters with Ambassador Anthony Biddle in Warsaw. When he left for Riga, Latvia, his next stop, he wrote his father a long report containing several misspelled words and the following conclusion: "Probably the strongest impression I have goten is that rightly or wrongly the Poles will fight over the Question of Danzig."

From Riga he flew to Moscow, and he noted that the Soviet plane had a windowpane missing and no passenger seats. His dispatch from Moscow declared that Stalin's Russia was "a crude, backward, hopelessly bureaucratic country." Jack also spent days in Leningrad and in the Crimea before moving on to Turkey and Palestine.

Torbert "Torby" Macdonald, Jack's roommate at Harvard and an all-American football player, came to Europe that summer, and for a while Jack traveled with him. On their drive from Paris to the Kennedy family villa at Cannes on the Riviera, their car overturned, but they escaped without injury. In Germany, the two joined Byron "Whizzer" White, another all-American football player from the University of Colorado, for a tour of Munich, the scene of the start of the Nazi movement. They were visiting the grave of one of the first Hitler followers when a gang of young Nazi hoodlums showered them with rocks on learning they were Americans. Whizzer and Torby wanted to wade in with punches, but Jack wisely talked them into leaving the scene.

Late in August, Alex Kirk, the U.S. chargé d'affaires in the American Embassy in Berlin, gave Jack a confidential message for his father: War would begin in a week. This proved correct, for on September 1, 1939, German tanks roared across the Polish border into the sun, and Nazi bomber planes dropped their explosive loads over Warsaw and other cities. As allies of Poland,

England and France then declared war on Germany on September 3, and World War II was on in earnest. It was on the following day that the first American involvement in the war took place. The British liner *Athenia,* carrying 300 Americans in its list of 1,400 passengers, was torpedoed by a German submarine while en route to Canada. When Ambassador Kennedy was informed that the 288 American survivors had been taken to Glasgow, Scotland, after almost a day adrift in lifeboats, he dispatched Jack and Eddie Moore, now his aide, to assist their countrymen.

On their arrival in Glasgow, Jack and Moore hurried to the hotel where the Americans were staying. Acting as spokesman for his father, Jack spoke to them reassuringly and promised to send an American ship to return them to the United States. Instead of being pleased, the rescued group turned angrily on him and demanded a convoy of American warships to protect them against further torpedoes. They drowned out the young diplomat, and he was forced to return to London to report a failure in his mission and to make a request that a Navy convoy guard the return home of the Americans.

By this time the Harvard school year had begun, and Jack ended his short diplomatic activities to return late to Cambridge. Because he had spent a semester in Europe, the Harvard administration ruled that he had to take extra courses if he wanted to graduate in June, 1940. This made it necessary for him to put in more time in the library. An additional factor in his growing seriousness toward his studies was his determination to graduate with honors in political science, his major subject.

Despite his previous poor academic record, Harvard permitted him to graduate with honors if he had a B average in his major and if he wrote a senior thesis paper. Jack gained his B standing in political science and wrote a thesis on the subject "Appeasement at Munich." The theme of his presentation was that British Prime Minister Chamberlain was not to be blamed for what was done at Munich. Instead, he wrote, the British people were at fault because of their opposition to rearmament and their desire to maintain a peaceful existence at home. This was the position taken by his father in dispatches from London to President Roosevelt, though his father went further by saying that at this late day England could no longer catch up with the military might of Nazi Germany.

Even with his burdensome course work and his long hours in Harvard's Widener Library, Jack found time for a host of side activities. He had added prestige, for Joe, who was now in law school, had sent George Taylor, his valet, to work for Jack. Taylor worried about the young man because he kept his room in chaotic disorder and ignored his large wardrobe by wearing the same clothes day after day—brown loafers, army khaki pants, and a rumpled tweed jacket. Jack was also playing the stock market and showed modest success after close watch of the financial papers and magazines. In addition, Jack, as a former on-the-scene observer, was in demand by fellow students for his opinions on current events. "I am quite a seer around here," he wrote his father. However, he would not join brother Joe in making speeches against American intervention in the European war.

Also pleasantly time-consuming were the many hours he spent with a girl with whom he had fallen in love. He never made public the girl's name, though his mother knew about it because he confided his sorrow to her when the romance ended. "He says she is the only one he really enjoyed going out with; and yet he admits that he did not want to get married," said Rose Kennedy.

In the spring of 1940, with his grades good and his thesis accepted, he won his degree with honors in political science. His father, forced to remain at his diplomatic post in London, sent the following cablegram to his son: TWO THINGS I ALWAYS KNEW ABOUT YOU ONE THAT YOU ARE SMART TWO THAT YOU ARE A SWELL GUY LOVE DAD.

Praise for his thesis by his professors had been so high that Jack wrote his father he would like to expand it and have it published as a book. Ambassador Kennedy liked the idea and enlisted the aid of Arthur Krock, a writer for the New York *Times* and a family friend. Krock found a literary agent for Jack, lined up a publisher, criticized the expanded manuscript chapter by chapter, and supplied the title. Krock's suggested title (which was used) was *Why England Slept.* This worried Jack because it was similar to *While England Slept,* the title of the last book by the new British Prime Minister, Winston Churchill. He wrote his father that he hoped Churchill would not be offended.

Ambassador Kennedy also devoted much time to Jack's book effort. "I have found several instances where you have misspelled names and got your dates wrong," he warned his son. In another letter, he criticized Jack for finding Chamberlain without blame for England's military weaknesses in September, 1938, when he met Hitler at Munich. It was the Prime Minister's task to educate the people on the needs of the times and to lead the way, said Kennedy. Jack assured him in reply that he would do no "white washing" of prime ministers. Kennedy also sent his son another letter in which he spelled out the means by which the United States could "profit by the lesson of England." Jack used this letter as the ending paragraphs of his book. Still another Kennedy service came when Arthur Krock expressed his willingness to write a preface to Jack's book. Kennedy thought a more important person should do this, and he won agreement from Henry Luce, the publisher of *Time* and *Life* to write the foreword.

*Why England Slept* was published in July, 1940, and it became a best seller and a Book-of-the-Month Club selection. Sales in the United States totaled 40,000, and an equal number were bought abroad. Jack used part of his American royalties to buy a new Buick, and he gave all his British royalties to the town of Plymouth, recently under heavy air bombardment by the Germans. Reviews of the book were mixed, though several important reviewers found it a significant work by someone surprisingly mature in his thinking at only twenty-three. What pleased Jack most was the pride of his father. The elder Kennedy gave copies to Churchill, Queen Mary, Harold Laski, and hundreds of others. To Jack he wrote: "You would be surprised how a book that really makes the grade with high-class people stands you in good stead for years to come."

Once the excitement of the book began to fade, Jack gave thought to his future. His first intention was to follow Joe into law, though he planned to attend Yale Law School and not Harvard, where Joe was enrolled. But toward the end of the summer he liked the idea of becoming a financial tycoon like his father, and he went to Palo Alto, California, to enter the Graduate School of Business at Stanford. Boredom set in by the end of the first semester, however, and in February, 1941, he went on a long tour of South America.

By the time he returned home Jack had decided to follow his brother Joe into the armed forces. However, his need for independence was still strong. When Joe went into Navy aviation, Jack tried to join the Army. Only after the Army rejected him because of the old football injury to his back did he attempt to become a naval officer. Again doctors at the Navy recruiting station found his back unfit for military duty and quickly rejected him. But Jack would not give up, and he spent the summer weight lifting and following a special diet to add pounds to his skinny frame. In September, 1941, he once more asked to be examined, and this time he passed the Navy's fitness test and was commissioned a lieutenant junior grade.

Jack Kennedy's first assignment took him to Washington. There he became an Intelligence officer in the office of the Chief of Naval Operations with the task of preparing a daily news summary. This displeased him because he wanted sea duty. After the Japanese attack on Pearl Harbor on December 7, he requested ship service. This brought him a change—assignment to a defense plant project in Charleston, South Carolina, to guard against sabotage and bombings. It was dull duty. After several months he appealed to his father to use his Washington connections to help him win a transfer to sea. Mr. Kennedy, who was no longer an ambassador, spoke to his friend Undersecretary of the Navy James V. Forrestal, and soon Jack was on his way to Portsmouth, New Hampshire, for training in motor torpedo boat (PT) training.

At Portsmouth and Newport Jack became so expert at handling the 80-foot PT boats that his instructors gave him a top grade in ship control. Later in 1942, he was sent to the Motor Torpedo Boat Squadron Training Center at Melville, Rhode Island, as a teacher. After instructions each day, he liked to put on his sweater with the crimson *H* stitched to it and wander to the cleared field for a game of touch football. Those not acquainted with him thought the "tall skinny kid" was from the local high school. Some who thought him a sissy at first glance found that once play started, they "saw nothing but elbows, shoulders and knees, and acquired a collection of bumps and bruises."

At last his naval training was put to use. In the winter of 1943 he received orders to board ship at San Francisco for duty in the South Pacific. In March, Shafty, as he was called, was given command of the torpedo boat PT-109 and a complement of twelve officers and men. American amphibious action was then in progress to regain control from the Japanese of the waters and islands of the Solomons and New Georgia, east of New Guinea.

PT-109's assigned task was to patrol the waters in that dangerous area and search out Japanese vessels. It was past midnight on August 2, 1943, when Lieutenant Kennedy on patrol ordered all engines except one cut off in order to proceed silently against Japanese ships that had been pounded the previous day by American bombers. The night air was heavy with haze and the sea rough, but in a momentary clearing Commander Kohei Hanami of the Japanese destroyer *Amagiri* caught sight of PT-109 and ordered his larger vessel to ram Kennedy's craft full speed.

By the time Kennedy became aware of what was happening he could not maneuver his ship out of danger because of its single operating engine. In a flash the onrushing *Amagiri* cut through the middle of PT-109 and continued on her way. The impact killed two Americans and slammed Kennedy on his already-weakened back onto the deck. When his mind partially cleared, he found his half of the ship was still afloat, and he saw four men clinging in the water to the hulk. Burning gasoline crackled the surface of the water as he called out in the dark to any other crewmen who might have survived. Six voices responded, and Kennedy swam around the fire to guide the men to the floating remains of PT-109.

In the morning, when help did not come and the mangled metal showed signs of sinking, Kennedy ordered his crew to swim to an island three miles away. One man had been severely burned, but Kennedy towed him in the five-hour swim by clamping his teeth onto the strap connected to the man's life jacket. Even after they struggled ashore, Kennedy would not rest. Dusk was falling when he swam to a nearby island and then out into Ferguson Passage, the normal patrol route of PT boats in the area. But no PT boats hove into sight. Sick and cut by coral reef, he returned to his men the next day.

## John Fitzgerald Kennedy

For four days after the meeting with the *Amagiri,* Kennedy kept his men on the move, for fear of being captured by the Japanese. At a point where the prospect of rescue seemed dim, Kennedy and Barney Ross, his third officer, swam to Nauru Island, close to Ferguson Passage. Two natives there fled at sight of the two bedraggled Americans. However, others came after a while to look at them, and Kennedy used his knife to write a message on a smooth coconut shell: ELEVEN ALIVE NATIVE KNOWS POSIT AND REEFS NAURU ISLAND KENNEDY. "Rendova, Rendova," he said to the natives, giving them the name of the island where some PT squadrons were stationed. One of the men picked up the coconut, and all left in their canoes.

He and Ross were sleeping the next morning on Nauru after a night of swimming in Ferguson Passage when a native awakened them. "I have a letter for you, sir," he told Kennedy. Rescue of all the men came shortly afterward. Back in the United States, Joseph Kennedy had received a telegram from the Navy Department informing him that Jack was missing in action. He did not tell his wife, and four days later she heard the story of Jack's survival on the radio. "They say Jack's been saved," she told her husband. "Saved from what?"

"Oh, nothing," he told her. Then to Jack he cabled: THANK GOD FOR YOUR DELIVERANCE!

Jack's war activities ended with the PT-109 incident. Shortly after his rescue, he became ill with malaria, and his weight fell to 120 pounds. In addition, the fall on the deck had brought on a recurrence of his old back injury, and the pain was sharp. Finally, in December, 1943, his overseas tour of duty came to an end, and he was ordered back to the United States.

For a few months, he seemed to be recovering as he worked as a PT boat instructor in warm Miami. But the pain in his back grew worse, and in May, 1944, he went into the Chelsea Naval Hospital, not far from Boston, for a spinal disk operation. He was at the family compound at Hyannis Port that day in August when word came of Joe's death. The shock to the entire family was tremendous. In the months that followed, Jack collected essays by Joe's friends and put them together in a book he called *As We Remember Joe*. He paid a publisher $5,000 to publish a few hundred copies of the book for distribution as Christmas presents that year. Twenty years later, dealers offered nearly $2,000 for each copy of *As We Remember Joe*.

In March, 1945, a Navy board pronounced Jack unfit for further service and ordered his retirement despite his improved health. At that time Germany teetered on the rim of total defeat and the Japanese war machine had only a few months of life left. The public was already talking about the postwar world, and there was excitement in the air over the conference to organize a United Nations, scheduled to begin on April 25 in San Francisco.

Once more a civilian, Jack became a reporter to cover the UN Charter Conference. Through his father's connections, the Hearst newspaper chain hired him to write "from a GI viewpoint," and he began a short career as a newsman at the very top. In San Francisco he soon had several private interviews with the heads of governments and foreign secretaries, he listened to the proceedings as the conference dragged on for nine weeks, and he chewed his pencil in the quiet of his hotel room as he pondered the significance of the emerging new international organization. His news stories cautioned against the view that all world problems were now to be solved on the parliamentary floor of the UN. He also wrote of the unfriendly attitude of the Soviet Union, the World War II ally of the United States, and reported that some conference delegates spoke "of fighting the Russians in the next ten or fifteen years."

After San Francisco, Jack wanted to do some reporting abroad and went to Europe. He was in England at the time of the general election; though the Conservative Party of Prime Minister Winston Churchill expected to win reelection without difficulty, Jack wrote that Churchill, the great war leader, could expect defeat. In Jack's view, Churchill was "fighting a tide that is surging through Europe, washing away monarchies and conservative governments everywhere." In the election, Churchill was shocked when the Labour Government of Clement Attlee swept him out of office.

Jack served also as a correspondent at the Potsdam Conference, the summit meeting between the Russian dictator Joseph Stalin, Attlee, and President Harry Truman, who had succeeded to the Presidency in April on the death of Franklin Roosevelt. There was much bickering between Stalin and Truman, who wanted to win Soviet agreement for a German peace treaty. In photos taken at this unsuccessful conference Jack Kennedy's thin face appeared along with those of political leaders in many of the pictures.

89

Following his return to the family home at Palm Beach, Florida, Jack Kennedy made a vital decision. After a few months as a newsman, he had come to the conclusion that reporting events was not as significant as participating in them. But if he were to be a participant, he would have to go into politics, and at twenty-eight he assessed himself as being shy, unhealthy, a poor speaker, too boyish in appearance, and in horror of slapping backs and acting like a "good fellow." Nevertheless, he decided that this was what he wanted to do despite his personal shortcomings. Later he was to say that he "went into politics because Joe died." And his father was quoted as confessing, "I got Jack into politics. I was the one. I told him Joe was dead and it was his responsibility to run for Congress. He didn't want to. He felt he didn't have the ability. . . . But I told him he had to." However, a more basic urge drove Jack Kennedy into politics. This was his desire to be a decision maker in the questions affecting his generation. Arthur Schlesinger, Jr., who would serve him in the White House, has written that his experience at the San Francisco Conference convinced him that he wanted a role in public life.

The first political possibility to open came with the offer by Governor Maurice Tobin of Massachusetts to take Jack on the ticket as his running mate for lieutenant governor in the next campaign. However, the elder Kennedy advised his son not to accept the offer because Tobin's popularity was declining. In addition, Joseph Kennedy believed a seat in Congress held a better political future.

James M. Curley, the seventy-year-old Boston boss and longtime foe of Honey Fitz, now presented the grandson of his old enemy with just the opportunity he sought. Curley had won election to Congress in 1942, but by 1945 he thirsted for the job as mayor of Boston, a post he had previously held for eight years. His desire proved so great that the Purple Shamrock, as he was called, ran in the mayorality contest and won another term in November, 1945.

This appeared to make Curley's Congressional seat available, for the law required that an election be held within ninety days to choose a successor to serve the rest of his term. But Curley refused to resign and held on to his House seat and salary throughout 1946, along with his position as mayor. As a result, Jack Kennedy had to wait until the spring of 1946 before he could announce himself as a candidate for the regular term beginning in January, 1947.

Curley's Congressional District was the Eleventh, a mixed area covering the slums of East Boston and the West and North End and then extending across the Charles River into a part of Somerville and the entire Harvard University town of Cambridge. At one end were the dilapidated three-story red-brick tenements teeming with the families of railroad workers, dockhands, teamsters, factory laborers, and the unemployed, At the other were the homes of Harvard scholars. Traditionally, this was a "safe" Democratic Congressional District. This meant that whoever won the June, 1946, Democratic primary was certain to win the general election the following November against the winner of the Republican primary.

When Jack returned to Boston to run for Curley's seat,

he felt the strangeness of having lived elsewhere for almost twenty years. On entering the Navy, he had listed Florida as his residence. In fact, on beginning his political career, he lacked a legal residence in Massachusetts. This he quickly remedied. Grampa Honey Fitz, now eighty-three and retired, lived with his wife in a suite at the Bellevue Hotel near the statehouse. Jack rented rooms a few floors away from Honey Fitz, which he proposed to use as his campaign headquarters and legal residence.

This solved one problem, but another arose that might have resulted in his disqualification as a candidate. The law required all persons running for office to have been a certified member of a political party for at least twenty days before April 30, the last day for filing as a candidate. Kennedy had never registered as a Democrat in Massachusetts and was not aware of this state law. However, one of his friends mentioned it to him on April 3, and he rushed that same day to City Hall to register and keep himself in the contest.

By the time the last filing day passed nine other Democrats had entered the race for Curley's Congressional seat. Newspapers agreed that the favorite was Mike Neville, the former mayor of Cambridge and state legislator. John Cotter, Curley's Congressional secretary, was also rated highly as a possible winner of the Democratic primary. Then there was Major Catherine Falvey, an officer in the WAC, who was expected to get the women's votes. A bit of confusion was supplied by two other candidates, each of whom was named Joseph Russo.

At the outset the line of the other candidates was to belittle Kennedy. Major Falvey labeled him "the poor little rich kid." Mike Neville condescendingly stated he would appoint Kennedy as his Congressional secretary. Others called him a carpetbagger who did not live in the Eleventh District.

Kennedy was not confident at the start of the primary campaign that he could overcome these attacks and win. In fact, he was not sure he had the ability to campaign. His first test came early. Francis X. "Frank" Morrissey, a young and likeable Boston Irishman and an aide to the elder Kennedy, had been assigned by Joseph Kennedy to teach Jack the art of professional politics. One day Morrissey, Joseph Kennedy, and Jack drove to Maverick Square, in the Italian ghetto of East Boston.

Morrissey parked the car across the street from a group of swarthy Sicilians who wore long black coats with upturned collars and big hats with the brims almost covering their dark eyes. Morrissey nodded, and Jack climbed out of the car, paused, and then crossed the street. He introduced himself to each man, shook his hand, and friendly smiles broke on their faces as he engaged them in conversation. "Everything's going to be fine," Morrissey exclaimed, letting out his breath happily. "I never knew Jack had it in him," gasped Joseph Kennedy in disbelief at the scene.

Jack had asked his Navy pals and Harvard friends to help him. They came from all parts of the country to address envelopes, answer telephones, arrange rallies, and knock on tenement doors. In addition to these enthusiastic amateurs, he surrounded himself behind the scenes with knowledgeable professionals, like Morrissey and Joe Kane, his father's cousin, who had spent forty years in Massachusetts politics.

As a man with a long political past, Grampa Honey

Fitz wanted to direct his grandson's campaign. But Jack's professional advisers pointed out that this would make a mockery of the candidate's campaign slogan of "The new generation offers a leader." So Honey Fitz remained quiet except on one occasion when Jack agreed to go with him to City Hall and let him introduce him to an assembly of city employees.

On their arrival, Honey Fitz immediately took the stage to sing "Sweet Adeline," and he asked the crowd to join him in several choruses. When the singing ended, Honey Fitz turned to his grandson and said, "Come on, Jack. Let's go."

"Grampa, did you forget?" asked Jack. "I'm the one running for office, not you."

"Oh, yes," Honey Fitz agreed. Then he turned back to the audience and announced that he wanted to introduce his grandson.

As the campaign progressed, Kennedy's opponents stopped sneering at him and grew worried. Instead of a rich young man's dawdling effort at campaigning, Kennedy was rising early each morning, donning a steel brace for his back, and then rushing through a hectic fourteen-hour day. Up and down the blocks of the Eleventh District he strode to shake hands and talk to people on the street and enter the rundown tenement buildings to meet voters. It was his first look inside tenements, and he was shocked by the mean living conditions he saw.

Each evening he also attended at least six house parties. These were arranged by his volunteers, who found one voter in each block who would act as a host in his home for his neighbors and Jack Kennedy. Coffee and cookies were served, and the candidate sat down to answer questions put to him. In cases where the host was too poor to handle the expense of a house party, the Kennedy volunteers furnished the dishes, silverware, flowers, and food. Despite his Harvard accent and boyish appearance, Jack surprisingly had no difficulty communicating with the people who came to these parties.

Jack's father worked almost as hard as Jack in the campaign. His advertising firm used billboards, postcards, and radio broadcasts to promote his son. The elder Kennedy also arranged to place four ads for Jack in every streetcar. Each ad carried an explanation by a longshoreman, a housewife, veteran, or businessman on "Why I Am for Jack Kennedy." Joseph Kennedy also kept close watch and criticized every aspect of the campaign. When the man who introduced Jack at rallies proved to be a far better speaker than his son, he had him removed. Still another action by Joseph Kennedy was to fly a highly regarded public opinion polling firm's personnel from New York to Boston to take sample polls on Jack's campaign. When these private polls showed that Jack's status as a war veteran was his biggest asset, Joseph Kennedy bought and distributed thousands upon thousands of copies of a *Reader's Digest* condensation of a *New Yorker* magazine article on the story of PT-109.

Joseph Kennedy also produced the biggest hit of the campaign. Engraved invitations went out to all voters in the Eleventh District to attend a formal reception and tea at the Hotel Commander to meet the candidate and his family. A large crowd of 1,500 came in formal clothes to walk through the receiving line and exchange a few words with the Kennedys. Joseph Kennedy came wearing his white tie and tails, and Rose Kennedy and the girls wore evening gowns.

All these efforts paid off on primary day, June 18, 1946. When the votes were counted, Jack Kennedy was far in front with 22,183, or almost as many as the total of his nine opponents. Mike Neville, in second place, had only about half of Jack's total. At the victory party that evening, Honey Fitz acted in character, singing "Sweet Adeline" and dancing an Irish jig on the table.

The election that November against Lester Bowen, his Republican opponent, proved to be the expected certainty for the Democrats. With his margin of more than two to one, Jack Kennedy entered the House of Representatives in January, 1947, for the first of three two-year terms.

These were six years that required little further campaigning. In 1948, for instance, he had no Democratic opponent in the primary, nor did the Republicans put up a candidate to run against him in the November general election. Then, in 1950, when he ran for his third two-year term, even though he had opponents in the primary and general election, his margin of victory in each was by five to one.

At the time he was sworn in as a member of the House, Kennedy was suffering from an attack of malaria. Speaker Sam Rayburn recalled that "when Kennedy came to the House, he had a swarthy, dark-yellowish complexion. It looked as if he had that Pacific fever. And he looked so spare." But when he recovered, he again looked so young that members of the House mistook him for a page. Once tourists on an elevator asked him to let them off on the fourth floor. Kennedy's appearance found favor with women reporters; one described him as being "six feet tall, broad-shouldered, and weighing 140 pounds, he has frank blue eyes, a shock of straight blond hair, perfect teeth, and freckles. He's so clean-cut, so typically American, you find yourself wishing Hitler could have seen this production of American youth."

When Kennedy first came to Washington, he set up bachelor quarters in a comfortable house in fashionable Georgetown, where a motherly housekeeper, servants, and a chauffeur looked after his needs. Every noon the chauffeur delivered a home-cooked meal to Kennedy's office in Thermos containers. He could always tell his employer from other Congressmen because Kennedy would be the only one not dressed in his best clothes. His usual attire in his first House term consisted of a wrinkled, old jacket, army khaki pants, and unpolished loafers—the clothes he had worn at Harvard. His sister Eunice lived with him for a time before she married and acted as his hostess when he gave parties. His mother, also a frequent visitor, nagged him without effect on the continuing untidiness of his bedroom and his clothes. In one of his early speeches on the House floor, his shirt-tail hung out. Another time he wore different-colored socks.

In the office, Kennedy was attentive to the needs of the people in his district, and his staff worked hard to get the veterans benefits and Social Security payments due them. "No one should represent a workingman's district who is not in sympathy with what the workingmen want," he said.

But beyond looking after the interests of his constituents and supporting President Truman's welfare legislation that would benefit the poor in his district, Kennedy revealed much of his father's conservatism. On domestic matters, he favored a sharp cutback in government spending and an extensive weakening of Presidential powers, while in foreign affairs he tended to be isolationist. In one speech he attacked the late President Roosevelt for the Yalta Agreement with Stalin, in which Roosevelt approved the postwar transfer of the Japanese Kurile Islands to the Soviet Union. In another speech, he lashed out at President Truman as being responsible for the fall of the Chiang Kai-shek government in China.

But in general, Kennedy made few speeches on the big issues, for he believed that individual House members below the level of committee chairmen had little influence on the direction of legislation. "We were just worms over in the House," he once said. "Nobody pays much attention to us nationally."

Yet Kennedy's independent manner that came from financial security, and the safe seat he held made it possible for him to move where other politicians were paralyzed. For instance, when the American Legion opposed the postwar public housing bill, many House members in favor of the legislation spoke of withdrawing their support because of the political power of the Legion in their Congressional Districts.

But Kennedy considered the Legion's action an outrage because veterans returning from the war faced a severe housing shortage. Rising on the House floor, he told his colleagues, "I am a member of the American Legion. I was never consulted." He then proceeded to attack the Legion's leaders for working with the real estate lobby, and he closed by saying, "The leadership of the American Legion has not had a constructive thought for the benefit of this country since 1918!"

Kennedy's speech brought gasps from listeners. Afterward members surrounded him and begged him to retract his statement for the sake of his political future. After listening in silence to this unanimous advice, Kennedy gained recognition from the Speaker for an additional statement. But instead of apologizing, he attacked American Legion officers even more harshly than before. When he returned to his office, he told Ted Reardon, his brother Joe's college friend and now Jack's chief aide, "Well, Ted, I guess we're gone." However, instead of the mail barrage of criticism, most of the letters supported his stand.

As his health improved, Kennedy found it impossible to spend long days sitting in his office swivel chair and on the hard benches in the House. His body required exercise, and on pleasant afternoons, he would speed home at three o'clock, change into sweater and old trousers, and then join touch football games at nearby playgrounds.

One afternoon he asked a local high school football coach if he could suit up and practice with the team. Seventeen-year-old halfback Freddy Greenleaf called to him as he ran onto the field, "Hey, kid, come over here and snag some passes." Kennedy did as he was told, and then the two exchanged punting the football to each other. "How's the Congressman doing, Freddy?" the coach asked.

"Is that what they call him?" Freddy asked. "He needs a lot of work. What year's he in?"

By 1950 Jack Kennedy found himself eager to move on to more exciting and powerful political posts. House members took note that after the House finished its business on Thursdays, he left Washington and did not return to the House benches until the following Tuesday. Many considered him a playboy more interested in social affairs and sailing than in his political duties.

However, when Kennedy left the capital on Thursdays, he flew to Boston, where Frank Morrissey met him at the airport with a chauffeur-driven limousine. Once Kennedy climbed into the back seat, they rode off across the state for three days of speechmaking and talks with local Democratic leaders.

By the time he could claim he had spoken at least once in each of Massachusetts' 350 towns and cities, professional politicians were convinced he intended to run for governor. This was actually his goal, for Governor Paul Dever, a popular Democrat, had confided to friends his interest in opposing U.S. Senator Henry Cabot Lodge in 1952. But when Lodge gained national publicity that year as the man who had induced General Dwight D. Eisenhower to run for President on the Republican ticket, Dever backed off and announced he would seek another term as governor. Kennedy then immediately told the press he planned to run for the Senate.

The first reaction generally was that Kennedy had blundered and would be retired from public life. Several newspapers played up the angle that Lodge's grandfather had defeated Honey Fitz in another Senate contest back in 1916, and they predicted a similar result for 1952. Lodge himself was bursting with self-confidence that he would easily win reelection to another six-year Senate term. Lodge advised Arthur Krock, of the New York *Times* and an old friend of the Kennedy's, that he "tell Joe not to waste his money on Jack because he can't win. I'm going to win by three hundred thousand votes." The elder Kennedy's reaction was to tell his son he was making the correct move. "When you've beaten Lodge," he told him, "you've beaten the best. Why try for something less?" Part of Joseph Kennedy's enthusiasm stemmed from the fact that he had been conducting private polls which revealed that Jack would do well against Lodge.

Jack had no opponent in the Democratic primary for his party's nomination. He considered this a handicap because he wanted to test his staff organization throughout the state. In addition, he believed that a period of political excitement in the spring would make the fall race easier against Republican Lodge. One test of his organization became available when he had to fulfill the law's requirement for the signatures of 2,500 registered voters on his nomination papers. To show his strength, Jack ordered his staff to collect 100 times this number. In short order they found 262,324 persons who willingly signed their names!

The Kennedy organization was like an army staff planning a military campaign. There were 286 Kennedy "secretaries" across the state who promoted him on the local scenes, and there were 20,000 volunteers to help them. Of great aid to them were the million copies of an eight-page paper focusing on the PT-109 episode that flooded the state. This paper contained the *Reader's Digest* reprint of the *New Yorker* article, several drawings of Jack rescuing his crew, and a photo of Joe with the story title "John Fulfills Dream of Brother Joe Who Met Death in the Sky over the English Channel." In addition to the local organizations and the newspaper, a large corps of speechwriters and advisers operated out of a small Boston apartment on Bowdoin Street that Jack had rented.

Despite the excellent organization and ample funds, the key to the campaign remained the candidate. Kennedy's handsome, clean-cut appearance gained him admirers wherever he traveled. He looked like a man in excellent health, and he spoke vigorously. Yet his physical condition was actually poor, for his back pain had recurred, more severely than before. Halfway through the campaign, he was forced to use crutches to keep his weight off his spinal base. His twenty-six-year-old brother Bobby, who served as his campaign manager, was aware of Jack's concern that he might have to quit campaigning. One campaign aide recalled, "He hated to appear in public on his crutches. When we came to the door of a hall where he was to make a speech, he'd hand the crutches to one of us and throw his shoulders back and march down the aisle as straight as a West Point cadet. How he did it, I'll never know."

By September the Kennedy campaign that had started off so well began to show signs of losing momentum. It had become apparent to both Kennedy and Lodge that their positions on domestic and foreign issues were so similar that they could never mount a meaningful debate of their differences. As a result, the campaign would have to be largely a popularity contest between two young, good-looking liberals of different parties and a promise by each to do more in office than the other.

This approach was soon revealed by their Battle of the Billboards. The Democratic candidate's billboards read: "Kennedy Will Do MORE for Massachusetts"; Lodge's signs boasted: "Lodge Has Done—and Will Do—the MOST for Massachusetts." After counting the number of signs for each candidate and judging their strategic locations, the Kennedy organization gleefully declared itself the winner of this battle.

Several factors now strengthened the Kennedy campaign. Republican Senator Joseph McCarthy of Wisconsin, who had spent two years in the national limelight irresponsibly charging that the national government was honeycombed with Communists, had said he would campaign in Massachusetts for Lodge. This would have been of great value to Lodge, for a large percentage of Massachusetts Democrats were McCarthy admirers. However, after Joseph Kennedy contributed money to McCarthy's reelection campaign, the Wisconsin Senator did not come to Massachusetts. In addition, the publisher of the influential but money-losing Boston *Post,* who had first come out for Lodge, switched his support to Kennedy a few weeks before election day. After the election, the elder Kennedy lent him $500,000 to keep his paper alive. Still another influential newspaper to change support to Kennedy was the New Bedford *Standard-Times.* The publisher had been a warm supporter of Senator Robert A. Taft for the Republican Presidential nomination the previous summer. When General Eisenhower won the nomination instead of Taft, he threw his newspaper behind Kennedy as punishment for Lodge, the keyman behind Eisenhower.

Still another important plus factor for Kennedy was

the help given him by his brothers, sisters, and mother. The girls and Rose Kennedy shook hands with tens of thousands of voters and held thirty-three formal receptions and teas for women voters. As in Kennedy's first campaign for his House seat, engraved invitations went to homes, as though a formal party at the best hotel were in store for card holders. The women who came in crowds to the receptions wore their best clothes to meet the Kennedys in their formal attire.

At each reception, Kennedy spoke briefly, pointing out that Lodge's grandfather had defeated his grandfather for the Senate "in an election where women were not allowed to vote. I hope that by impressing the female electorate," he concluded, "that I can more than take up the slack." Then he would invite each woman present to meet him, his mother, and his sisters and have a cup of tea with the Kennedys.

The Kennedy girls also rang thousands of doorbells, took part in an uncounted number of house parties, and were featured in two TV specials, *Coffee with the Kennedys*. But it was Rose Kennedy who was an even more important asset for her son in the Boston area. The North End where she had been born was now an Italian ghetto; she was heartily applauded when she spoke a few sentences in Italian and proceeded to tell how she had reared nine children. At meetings in higher income areas, she wore expensive jewelry and a mink stole. Following her short talk of praise for her son, she was cheered when she said, "Now let me tell you about the new dresses I saw in Paris last month."

In the early returns on election night, at first Lodge

led, then Kennedy. After midnight, sadness swept through Kennedy's headquarters because Lodge was ahead. Advisers were concerned that Lodge would win election on the coattails of General Eisenhower, who was defeating Adlai E. Stevenson in the state by more than 200,000 votes. But the Lodge lead melted away during the night and by 6 A.M., when Kennedy's margin over Lodge was 70,000 with 2,350,000 votes cast, Lodge publicly conceded Kennedy had defeated him.

"At last, the Fitzgeralds have evened the score with the Lodges," said Rose Kennedy, saddened only because Honey Fitz had not lived long enough to enjoy this moment. As for Lodge, he bluntly said his defeat had resulted from "those tea parties."

When Kennedy came to the Senate in January, 1953, the Republicans, led by Senator Taft of Ohio, held numerical control of the upper house. This meant that they ran the machinery of the Senate, held the chairmanship of all committees, and had a majority on each committee.

Kennedy had hoped to play an important part in the Senate from the start, but with the Democrats in the minority this was not possible. Nor was he able to convince Democratic Minority Leader Lyndon Johnson to give him a seat on the Senate Foreign Relations Committee. Instead, Johnson put him on the Government Operations Committee, where Senator Joseph McCarthy was chairman, and on the Education and Labor Committee.

His failure to get on Foreign Relations was a disappointment to Kennedy, for this was his chief interest. For instance, in 1951, he had gone to Europe for six weeks at his own expense to talk to leaders of governments about their problems. Then, that autumn, he made a trip around the world, halting for "study stops" in various Middle East countries, India, Pakistan, French Indochina, Malaya, and Korea. In long reports, he had found the caliber of American foreign service personnel to be poor, he opposed the Korean War, and he angered French officials in Indochina by urging the end of French colonization and the grant of independence to their Vietnamese, Laotian, and Cambodian subjects.

On the Senate floor, Kennedy's lack of seniority put him in the back row of desks on the Democratic side of the aisle. As a rule, a new Senator was expected to be silent his first year. However, on May 18, 1953, after only four months, Kennedy made his first speech, choosing for his subject the economic problems of New England. It was his intention to impress his Senate colleagues and also to gain national newspaper attention. When he finished, Senator Hubert Humphrey, who occupied the desk next to him, graciously congratulated him. But few others did. Nor did the New York *Times* mention his speech.

Nevertheless, Kennedy's first major test as a legislator brought him widespread approval. Massachusetts politicians had campaigned in opposition to the construction of the St. Lawrence Seaway on the ground that it would destroy the profitable operation of the Port of Boston. In his 1952 campaign, Kennedy had agreed with this view. But when the bill came to a vote in the Senate, he took the position in a speech that the seaway would benefit the entire nation, and he voted for it.

That first year he was a Senator, a profound change

took place in his personal life. Back in early 1951, a reporter friend had arranged a dinner party in Washington with the purpose of acting as a matchmaker. Invited to his party were Kennedy and a college girl, who, at twenty-one, was twelve years younger than he. The girl was Jacqueline Lee Bouvier, who lived in nearby Arlington and had been reared as a Catholic in a socially prominent and wealthy family. She had gone to private schools, Vassar, and the Sorbonne in Paris, and she was now in her senior year at George Washington University.

Jack enjoyed her company at the party, but following that first meeting, he did not call her for a date until six months later. After that, he saw her regularly, said Jacqueline, although their dates had to fit in with his schedule of weekend speaking trips to Massachusetts. "He'd call me from some oyster bar up there," she once admitted, "to ask me out to the movies the following Wednesday in Washington." The movies were either Civil War films or Westerns.

Arthur Krock found a job for her after graduation as an inquiring camera girl with the Washington *Times-Herald* at a salary of $42.50 a week. Her job was to pick a question for the day, ask people on the street to answer it, photograph them, and write up the answers to run in the paper with the pictures. This kept her occupied during much of 1952, a period during which Kennedy was too busy running against Lodge to be a steady suitor.

But once he came to Washington as a Senator, he saw her more frequently, and they went to movies, parties, and Virginia fox hunts. Finally, in June, 1953, they announced their engagement, and they were married on September 12, 1953, after the Congressional session ended. Archbishop Richard Cushing officiated at the ceremony at Newport, Rhode Island, brother Bobby was best man, and the police had difficulty controlling the crowd of several thousand who stood outside the church for a glimpse of the handsome couple.

The newlyweds had hardly moved into their $125,000 house in the Virginia hills when Kennedy's back began paining him more sharply than ever before. He had also suffered another attack of malaria shortly before the wedding, and this had left him weak. In addition, he was bothered by an adrenal insufficiency that made him susceptible to infections and shock.

By the spring of 1954 he required crutches in order to walk. In his office he could not sit on a regular chair but had to use a rocker, and at home he was forced to sleep on a board. Special tests that summer at Boston's Leahy Clinic revealed that if nothing were done, he would become permanently crippled. An operation was possible, but chances that he would survive were slight. On being told this, he insisted on the operation. "I'd rather die than spend the rest of my life as a cripple," he informed a doctor.

With the Senate in recess, Kennedy entered Manhattan's Hospital for Special Surgery in October, 1954. He lay on the operating table for several hours while surgeons completed a delicate double fusion of spinal disks. Then he was wheeled back to his room to lie flat on his back in a dark room for weeks, with blood tests administered every half hour and with frequent blood transfusions. Two times doctors believed he was near death and summoned his wife and family to his bedside where he received the last rites of the Catholic church. But he did not die, even though the surgical opening in his back would not stop draining.

In December doctors, noting his lack of progress, thought he might recover in the warmth of Florida. So he was carried on a stretcher to a plane and was delivered to his father's house in Palm Beach. In February, 1955, doctors ordered him back to New York for another operation. Again he emerged from surgery close to death, and once more priests administered last rites. However, not only did he survive but at the end of the month surgeons removed the plate that had been inserted in his spine and said he could return to Florida to recuperate.

While Kennedy lay in bed recuperating during the next few months, he used the period to excellent advantage. His father said later, "Jack couldn't sleep for more than an hour at a time, because his pain was so bad. So he'd study to get his mind off the pain. That's where the book came from."

Kennedy conceived of writing a book that would tell how eight men in public life showed great political courage under circumstances that endangered their political futures. Friends and historians suggested men he should include in the book. Arthur Krock, for instance, argued that he must give a chapter to Senator Robert Taft, who defied popular opinion by opposing the Nuremberg trial of leading Nazis after World War II.

From Washington, the Library of Congress sent case after case of history books to Palm Beach. In addition, Kennedy's assistant, Theodore "Ted" Sorensen, dispatched packages of research notes and first drafts of various chapters. Others who sent first drafts were Jules David, professor at Georgetown University, and James

Landis, former head of Harvard Law School and Kennedy family lawyer.

Kennedy went over the material sent him, incorporated material from his own readings, and then rewrote the chapters. Afterward Professor Allan Nevins, renowned historian who taught at Columbia University, prepared a criticism of Kennedy's second draft and also wrote a foreword.

*Profiles in Courage,* as the book was titled, proved to be an immediate best seller after its publication in 1956. The following year it won the Pulitzer Prize. Of vital importance to his political career, it pushed him into the national limelight as no activity as a Senator could have achieved for him.

The regard which the U.S. Senate had for its second youngest member was revealed on May 24, 1955, when he returned to the Senate chamber for the first time since the previous October. His legs were shaky, his shoulders were high and rigid, and he walked with a limp into the chamber. On sight of him, the Senate stopped its work, and all present rose and applauded. "We are glad to have you back, Jack," Senator Lyndon Johnson said in behalf of his colleagues. In his office, Kennedy found a large basket of fruit with a card reading: "Welcome home." The signature of the sender was "Dick Nixon," the Vice President. The next day the recurring pains were so bad that he went to a doctor in New York for the first of a long series of injections of novocaine.

Although Kennedy had promised his wife he would follow the doctor's orders and rest for several months after his return to the capital, he was soon deeply involved in politics. In the Senate, he led the opposition to a proposed change in the electoral college, which he believed was even more undemocratic than the method set forth in the Constitution to choose American Presidents. In Massachusetts, he took on the Democratic Party's state organization because it opposed the renomination of Adlai Stevenson for President. After a long bitter fight, he was successful in defeating and ousting William "Onions" Burke, the chairman of the State Democratic Committee. However, Congressman John McCormack defeated the effort by Kennedy to pledge the state delegation to the national convention to support Stevenson in 1956.

On the national scene, Kennedy set his sights on his party's Vice Presidential nomination. Since Presidential nominees customarily chose their running mates and then had the convention endorse their choice, Kennedy thought he had the Vice Presidential nomination when Stevenson asked him at the opening of the August, 1956, convention to make the important speech nominating him for President. However, after Stevenson was renominated, he announced that the convention was free to select his running mate.

All night long Kennedy and his aides raced from one state delegation to another to win support. From France, where he was vacationing, Joseph Kennedy went without sleep as he placed phone calls to convention leaders in Chicago.

On the first ballot the next day, Senator Estes Kefauver of Tennessee was in front with 483½ votes to 304 for Kennedy, with votes going to several others. On the second ballot, Kennedy shot ahead of Kefauver, 618 to 551½, with 686 votes necessary to win. The third bal-

111

lot showed Kennedy's total rising to 648, and his nomination seemed near as chairmen of several delegations waved their state banners to win recognition from Chairman Sam Rayburn. At this crucial point, Congressman John McCormack yelled, "Sam! Sam! Missouri!"

Rayburn gave the floor to Missouri, and the state delegation announced it was shifting its votes to Kefauver. A roar went up, and other delegations switched to Kefauver. Before the roar died, Kefauver won the nomination.

Kennedy afterward tried to find good in his own defeat. "If my brother Joe had lived," he told a reporter, "he would have gone on in politics and he would have been elected to the House and Senate as I was. And, like me, he would have gone for the Vice-Presidential nomination at the 1956 convention. But, unlike me, he wouldn't have been beaten. Joe would have won the nomination. And then he and Stevenson would have been beaten by Eisenhower, and today Joe's political career would be in shambles and he would be trying to pick up the pieces."

After Adlai Stevenson's defeat by President Eisenhower in 1956, Jack Kennedy took careful note of his own political future. He might try to run again for the Vice Presidential nomination in 1960, or he could attempt to become a Senate "great." There was yet another possibility: Why not seek the Presidency? As he put it, it required as much effort to run for Vice President as for President. So it was foolish to try for second place instead of the nation's highest political honor.

In December, 1956, a month before President Eisenhower's second inauguration, Kennedy began his four-year labor to become Eisenhower's successor in January, 1961. Accompanied by Ted Sorensen, his speechwriting aide, he set out across the country in crisscrossing travels to make himself well known to the nation and local political leaders. He seldom sat at his desk in Room 362 of the Senate Office Building, for his competent staff was available to handle the Washington problems of Massachusetts citizens. Nor was he often found at his desk in the Senate chamber to take part in debate or promote bills.

Instead, he was traveling from state to state and town to town, to shake thousands of hands, make hundreds of speeches, and appear on TV. In one six-week swing, he spoke in twenty-four states and gave 150 speeches. He talked to labor conventions, farm groups, business and civic organizations, state legislatures, state fairs, university convocations, high school assemblies, lodge meetings, and bar associations, and at every stop he met the local press for interviews. Sorenson recalled those years on the move: "He slept in countless hotels and motels, some shabby, in governors' mansions and private homes and frequently all night on a plane."

While other Presidential hopefuls watched with growing concern, Kennedy became the object of a huge publicity campaign. Almost all leading magazines ran articles on him, and national TV shows interviewed him repeatedly. He came across on television as a handsome man, much younger in appearance than his age of forty in 1957, he spoke earnestly about the nation's problems, and he sounded like an intellectual who read and thought a great deal. Said his father proudly: "Jack is the greatest attraction in the country today. Why is it that when his picture is on the cover of *Life* or *Redbook* that they sell a record number of copies? You advertise the fact that he will be at a dinner and you will break all records for attendance."

Throughout 1957 the Kennedy organization was gaining experience in smooth operations, and his candidacy was growing stronger with each passing week. But then came 1958 and with it a possible cause for ending his chances for the Presidency. He faced a reelection contest for his Senate seat that year, and he knew he had to defeat Vincent J. Celeste, his Republican opponent, by half a million votes or be laughed off as a poor vote getter.

Celeste was not in a mood to make Kennedy's task easy. A hard-hitting campaigner, he charged Kennedy with being a puppet of his father and declared he had voted for the St. Lawrence Seaway solely because "it starts right at the front door of the Merchandise Mart in Chicago, which is owned by old Joe Kennedy." Celeste also hammered away on the theme that Kennedy was a millionaire who could not understand the lives and hopes of those not as fortunate as he. Still another Celeste attack centered on Kennedy's cross-country trips, which, he said, showed he had no interest in his Senate job.

As for Kennedy, he campaigned hard, relying on his warm smile, firm handshake, short talks, and the goodwill created since 1953 by the attentiveness of his large Senate staff to the requests from local citizens. In the last few weeks of the campaign, he was on the go almost around the clock, fearful that he might not attain the magic margin of 500,000 votes. Election day finally came, and his lead of 874,608 votes over Celeste pushed him farther along the road toward the Presidency.

By 1960 Kennedy had become so strong a contender for his party's nomination that other candidates began attacking him. They said privately and publicly that he had not paid attention to his Senate responsibilities, that he could not win because he was a Catholic, and that he was too young and lacked any experience as an executive. Despite such attacks, the public opinion polls revealed him to be ahead in popularity of Senators Lyndon Johnson, Stuart Symington, and Hubert Humphrey, as well as Adlai Stevenson, who were considered his chief rivals.

By custom, candidates delayed making a public announcement that they were running for the Presidency as long as they could. A chief reason for this was the desire to concentrate the enthusiasm for their candidacy in the final few months before the convention began. Kennedy's formal announcement came on January 2, 1960, as though he did not want to waste time acting the role of a coy candidate. Furthermore, he taunted all others, who were pretending they were not candidates, to join him in the Presidential primaries in the spring of 1960.

There was danger in the primaries for Kennedy if all the candidates competed. The convention votes to be gained in the primaries were only a small part of the total, for only a dozen states held primaries. In the other states, party leaders selected delegates to the convention. Yet the primary was the sole direct test of a candidate's popularity, and if Kennedy should lose a few, he would be seriously weakened.

Joy came to the Kennedy camp when Adlai Stevenson refused to run in any primary. Stevenson's intention was to have the national convention draft him for his third Presidential nomination. There was also pleasure when Johnson and Symington declared they would not enter the primaries. Johnson realized he would not win a single Northern primary because he was a Southerner, and this was his chief consideration. However, he could have defeated Kennedy in the West Virginia primary, for Democrats in this border state favored him, according to Kennedy's private public opinion polls. Had Johnson entered even this single primary after Kennedy announced he would, the effect of a Johnson victory would have probably finished Kennedy as a Presidential candidate.

However, Johnson chose not to do so, and only Senator Humphrey, the weakest of the Presidential contenders, entered the primary races against Kennedy. Even here, Humphrey limited himself to competition in Wisconsin and West Virginia, where newspaper editors considered him popular. As for Kennedy, he entered these primaries, plus six others in which no major candidate opposed him. Wisely, he decided against running in California and Ohio, where popular local Democrats would have defeated him.

Because Wisconsin and West Virginia were the sole tests for Democratic candidates, newspapers, magazines, and TV networks gave these two contests enormous coverage. In Wisconsin Kennedy won 56 percent of the vote, too small a margin to claim he had overwhelming popular support. In West Virginia both Kennedy and Humphrey campaigned as though the other held an immense advantage. By tradition, West Virginia voters were said to oppose office holding by Catholics, and wherever he spoke, Kennedy repeated his plea that religious prejudice be ended. As for Humphrey, he concentrated his attack on Kennedy's wealth and said that the large amount of money his opponent was spending in his campaign made the contest unfair. Humphrey said he felt like the small independent druggist who watched a large drug chain move in across the street. Finally, on May 10, 1960, the primary race ended with the statewide casting of ballots. Kennedy's victory was decisive: He had won 61 percent of the votes and led in forty-eight of fifty-five counties in the Mountain State.

When the Democratic National Convention opened in Los Angeles on July 11, the Kennedy forces were confident of victory. A count of delegates showed Kennedy had been promised the votes of about half the total. (He needed one more than half, or 761 votes, to win.)

Closest to him was Senator Johnson, with the backing of about 400 delegates. In an effort to gain on Kennedy, Johnson attacked his record as a Senator, pointing to the many votes he had missed because of his campaigning and charging that he had fathered few pieces of significant legislation. Johnson's aides went far beyond their employer and spread the false rumor that Kennedy was afflicted with an incurable disease and was kept alive only by daily injections of cortisone.

Tension ran high as the first ballot got under way at 10 P.M. on July 13. As the states were called in alphabetical order, some Kennedy advisers grew worried by reports that if Kennedy did not win on the first ballot, a large number of delegates planned to desert him on the second.

After Wisconsin voted, Kennedy's total stood at 748, or 13 below the needed 761. Only Wyoming was left, and when that state was called, the convention hall fell stone silent. Then a wild uproar developed after the chairman of the delegation shouted, "Mr. Chairman, Wyoming casts all fifteen votes for the next President of the United States—John F. Kennedy!"

The effort that had begun in December, 1956, had succeeded, and Kennedy was now the Presidential nominee of the Democratic Party. On the following day he selected Lyndon Johnson as his running mate, in order to pick up Southern votes in the November general election. Then, on Friday evening, July 15, he addressed the convention.

This was a speech in which he first mentioned the theme of his administration, should he be elected President. The theme was "The New Frontier," and he said: "Too many Americans have lost their way, their will and their sense of historic purpose. . . . Some would say . . . that all the horizons have been explored . . . that there is no longer an American frontier . . . the New Frontier of which I speak . . . holds out the promise of more sacrifice instead of more security. . . . Beyond that frontier are uncharted areas of science and space, unsolved problems of peace and war, unconquered pockets of ignorance and prejudice, unanswered questions of poverty and surplus."

Once the Republicans selected Vice President Richard M. Nixon as their Presidential nominee and former Senator Henry Cabot Lodge as his running mate, the

1960 campaign for the White House began. It ended three months later after Kennedy and Nixon each had made more than 500 speeches and traveled through almost all the states.

Early in the campaign, Kennedy took an important step to combat opposition to his candidacy because he was a Catholic. In mid-September, he went to Houston, Texas, where he addressed the Ministerial Association of Protestants and answered questions members asked. The TV coverage of the event gained him national attention on this vital matter. "I believe in an America where the separation of church and state is absolute," he declared. If he were elected President, he explained, no officer of the Roman Catholic Church would tell him how to act. At the same time, he added, he would expect "no Protestant minister would tell his parishioners for whom to vote." The applause that greeted his statement gave indication that the issue of his religion would no longer be a major factor in the election.

At the outset, Kennedy realized that another deficit he faced was the fact that Mr. Nixon was better known than he because he had served two terms as Vice President under President Eisenhower. Nixon would have been wise to campaign in the established fashion of delivering speeches over radio and TV and from back platforms of trains. Instead, he blundered by agreeing to take part in four TV debates with his Democratic opponent.

This was an error because it added to Kennedy's publicity by bringing his name to the attention of people who were ordinarily not interested in listening to a Democratic candidate. In addition, if Nixon won the debates, said the experts, he would add few voters to his side, but if Kennedy bested him, Nixon would probably lose millions of supporters.

The first debate was the most important of the four, and it proved to be a catastrophe for the Republican. The studio wall was gray, and so was Nixon's suit. A man who always dressed well, he came wearing a shirt with a collar a full size too large for his neck. Then there was the makeup man who tried to conceal Nixon's heavy beard with a deep overlayer of powder. So he seemed to fade into the walls, his neck looked scrawny, and under the bright lights his facial powder made him appear ill. Furthermore, he did not answer as quickly and energetically as Kennedy, and when the debate ended, Kennedy had taken a giant stride in his campaign.

Besides his success in handling the religious issue and the debates, Kennedy was aided by two other Nixon mistakes. In order to show he was self-reliant and independent, Nixon had not asked President Eisenhower to campaign for him until the final week before the election. Eisenhower aides have said that the general was eager to campaign for Nixon and was annoyed because he was not asked to do so. Eisenhower's great popularity could have added many votes to his total. Another mistake was Nixon's failure to telephone Mrs. Martin Luther King, Jr., whose husband had been arrested in Atlanta, Georgia, for leading a restaurant sit-in. Kennedy's sympathetic phone call to Mrs. King won him support from Negro leaders.

There was more to the campaign than Nixon's errors. On the positive side, Kennedy drew generous support when he promoted the idea of his New Frontier. The

John Fitzgerald Kennedy

cheers were also loud when he mentioned his campaign slogan: "It's time for America to start moving again." On the campaign trail, teen-age girls in the towns and cities he passed through had made him their idol, and their actions at the sight of him added much to the excitement. Kennedy classified them by types and called them his "jumpers," "double-jumpers," "touchers," "grabbers," and "roadrunners."

November 8, 1960, was the day of reckoning for both exhausted candidates. Across the country more than 68,000,000 people were to cast their ballots before the polls closed that night. After the long campaign, an assistant took note of its physical effect on Kennedy: "His hand was wrenched, scratched, swollen and infected. His face was creased with lines that had not been there a year before."

Early returns put Kennedy in the lead, but by 10 P.M. he and Nixon were running neck and neck. At 4 A.M., with the election still undecided, Kennedy was so tired that he went to bed. At 9 A.M. an aide climbed the stairs to the second-floor Kennedy bedroom in his Hyannis Port house. "Congratulations, Mr. President," he greeted Kennedy.

Out of the total votes cast, Kennedy had 34,221,463 to Nixon's 34,108,582, for a tiny lead of only 112,881. But in the electoral college, where the winner in a state wins the state's entire electoral vote, Kennedy emerged far ahead with a total of 303 to Nixon's 219. Joseph Kennedy, who had kept count all night of the popular and electoral vote, was overjoyed when Nixon sent his son a telegram at noon conceding defeat. "Jack doesn't

121

belong any more to just a family," he proudly told a reporter. "He belongs to the country."

John F. Kennedy had seventy-three days from the time of his election until he took office for resting, selecting his Cabinet and hundreds of other top officials, and preparing a program for his administration. These ten weeks passed swiftly, and suddenly it was January 20, 1961, his inauguration day.

Eight inches of snow that had fallen on Washington the night before were cleared from the main avenues and the Capitol Plaza, where viewers would witness the swearing in of the new President. At 12:51 P.M., with the day raw and the wind blowing angrily, the youngest man ever to be elected President took his oath of office from Chief Justice Earl Warren. Then, in his inaugural address, he sounded a call to the country that would henceforth be associated with his name: ". . . my fellow Americans, ask not what your country can do for you: Ask what you can do for your country." Old classmates at Choate recalled that the headmaster, Dr. St. John, had frequently told them: "Ask not what your school can do for you: Ask what you can do for your school."

Later on that triumphant day, he rode down Pennsylvania Avenue to the White House to review the hourslong parade. That night he, his wife, Jacqueline, and their two children, three-year-old Caroline and infant son, John, Jr., slept for the first time in the 132-room Executive Mansion.

As the Kennedy administration began, political observers predicted a brilliant two-term Presidency for the forty-three-year-old Chief Executive. A large number of young people had flocked to Washington to staff government agencies, and their energy and enthusiasm came to denote the new administration. Such energy was also characteristic of the President, who sent fifty special messages and requests for legislation to Congress in his first hundred days in office. One of these bills called for the establishment of a Peace Corps so that thousands of Americans could volunteer to live in backward countries and teach skills to the natives.

The new administration also made culture an important part of its activities. Outstanding musicians and dancers performed at White House functions, and artists and writers were regularly invited to dinner. In addition, Mrs. Kennedy took on the task of restoring the White House to its earlier splendor by acquiring the furniture and other belongings used there by previous occupants. Most of all, Mrs. Kennedy sought pieces that had once belonged to early-nineteenth-century residents, such as James Madison and James Monroe.

The first break in the successes of the new administration came on April 17, 1961, less than three months after the inauguration. In the final period of the Eisenhower administration, the CIA had begun to train Cuban exiles in Guatemala for an invasion of their homeland, in order to free Cuba from the Communist regime of Fidel Castro, who had gained control in 1958. By destroying the Castro government, the CIA hoped to end the fear of Cuba's neighbors of Communist subversion.

Shortly after Kennedy became President, the head of the CIA, top Army and Navy officers, Secretary of State Dean Rusk, and Secretary of Defense Robert McNamara urged him to go ahead with the liberation plan. All said that when the band of 1,400 invaders reached the beaches at the Bay of Pigs, the entire country would rise up to join them.

With the weight of such advice, Kennedy agreed to the invasion, and he gave the signal for its start. On April 15, eight American B-26's with Cuban pilots took off from Nicaragua to bomb the three main Castro airfields, in order to make the landings safe two days later. However, on the seventeenth the 1,400 were met not only by Castro's large army in the marshlands of the Bay of Pigs but also by planes from the airfields that were supposed to have been destroyed. Furthermore, the expected rise of the Cuban people against Castro did not take place.

Kennedy's advisers now clamored for more air strikes, this time by the U.S. Air Force, to save the unlucky 1,400 Cubans. Some asked for an invasion of Cuba by American armed forces.

But Kennedy saw that such actions would turn his administration into one with a reputation for seeking war as a solution to international problems. As he ordered the invasion ended, leaving the 1,400 to their fate, a White House aide said, "This is the first time that Jack Kennedy ever lost anything."

The Bay of Pigs fiasco taught Kennedy two important lessons. One was that he had to depend on his own judgment and not on the enthusiastic advice of military men. The other was that there was more to be gained from aiding Castro's neighbors to raise their living standards and develop democratic institutions to withstand Communism.

Since 1945 the United States and the Soviet Union had engaged in a cold war around the globe. To probe whether the Communists were interested in lessening international troubles, Kennedy went to Vienna in June, 1961, for a face-to-face meeting with the Soviet dictator Nikita Khrushchev. Along the way, he stopped first in Canada; then he and Mrs. Kennedy went on to Paris for political talks with President Charles de Gaulle of France. There were many glittering parties and receptions for the Kennedys in Paris, and Mrs. Kennedy was so warmly applauded wherever they appeared that at one point Kennedy described himself as "the man who accompanied Jacqueline Kennedy to Paris."

The meetings with Krushchev proved unpleasant. The Communist leader threatened a new crisis over Berlin by the end of the year, and Kennedy's reply was a firm "It is going to be a cold winter." Later Kennedy sent 50,000 American troops to Germany to show that he would not permit the Communists to push the United States out of West Berlin. However, he would not be goaded into war, as some advisers requested, when the Communists erected their Berlin Wall.

The greatest problem with the Soviet Union was not to occur in Berlin. It developed in Cuba. The crisis point was reached on October 16, 1962, when American reconnaissance planes flying over Cuba photographed Soviet missiles on Cuban launching sites. These missiles, equipped with nuclear warheads, were capable of destroying the southern half of the United States.

During the next four days Kennedy met with the executive committee of the National Security Council to determine his course of action. Some members, including Vice President Johnson, favored an all-out military invasion and occupation of Cuba. Others proposed holding immediate discussions with the Soviet leaders to demand the removal of the missiles. Still others advocated a blockade of Cuba so that no further military supplies could reach Castro.

Day after day, following the first newspaper stories of the crisis, the probability of a nuclear war between the world's two strongest powers seemed close at hand. Across the United States, people began digging bomb shelters in their backyards and stocking them with food and water. Others made plans to leave big-city areas.

All this time, Kennedy carefully weighed his alternatives. Finally, he made his decision and announced it publicly in a TV address: The United States would establish a sea and air blockade of Cuba so that no military supplies would reach Castro; any missile launched from the island against the United States would be considered a Soviet attack and would lead to retaliation against the Soviet Union.

Now it became Khrushchev's turn to react. His first response was to label the blockade American piracy. Nevertheless, when Communist ships en route to Cuba were met by American naval vessels, they stopped their engines and did not proceed until they were inspected and given permission. Then, on October 26, a letter from the Soviet dictator reached Kennedy's desk: Khrushchev would withdraw his missiles under UN inspection if Kennedy agreed not to invade Cuba. When Kennedy approved these terms, the worst crisis of his administration ended.

Besides his series of continuing crises with Communist nations, Kennedy involved his administration in many far-reaching activities involving the home front. His New Frontier theme called for combating racial discrimination, making war on poverty, providing decent medical care for the aged, improving the quality and quantity of education, eliminating ghettos, holding down inflation, and reforming the tax structure to make it fair.

These proposals ran immediately into the opposition of a conservative Congress unwilling to move swiftly into new areas. Some advisers argued with Kennedy that he denounce Congress, but he chose instead to follow a quotation of Thomas Jefferson that "great innovations should not be forced on slender majorities." Although the Democrats occupied most seats in the House and Senate chambers, Kennedy was aware that many Democrats did not fear Presidential anger because they represented "safe" districts and states, just as he had as a Congressman.

As a result, he showed patience in convincing independent members of Congress and powerful committee chairmen that his measures were necessary for the continued democratic growth of the nation. This meant going through repeated committee hearings on his bills and promoting them at his Presidential news conferences and through speeches to the people. It also meant an endless number of meetings with House and Senate members in his Oval Office to discuss the merits of his proposals.

In addition, Kennedy made use of private groups to help bring the New Frontier into being. For instance, he met in June, 1963, with leaders of Negro organizations to discuss a dramatic appeal to the nation and Congress for the passage of his civil rights legislation. The outcome was the Civil Rights March on Washington on

August 28 by a quarter of a million persons. The dignity of the marchers and the eloquence of Dr. Martin Luther King, Jr., so impressed the nation that the chances were boosted sharply that Congress was now ready to end discrimination in hotels and restaurants and provide equal voting rights for all Americans.

By late 1963 Kennedy felt he had come a long way. Congressional leaders agreed that the major bills of his New Frontier, still not acted upon, would at last become law during the next session of Congress. In addition, public opinion polls showed that his tiny margin of victory in 1960 over Richard Nixon had now grown into substantial popularity in all sections of the country except the South. There several pockets of bitter antagonism still remained, chiefly because of his civil rights stand, though Southern moderates were becoming less afraid to voice their support of the President.

A Kennedy dynasty seemed in the making to reporters that fall, for his two younger brothers, Bobby and Teddy, were by then being mentioned as his successors as President when he finally left office. Angry opponents were charging that news about the doings of the Kennedys filled the pages of the daily papers and pushed aside other happenings: Mrs. Kennedy, Caroline, and John were fully covered in the society edition, and the three Kennedy brothers in the front pages.

There appeared to be some substance to the talk about a Kennedy dynasty. The two younger brothers were already making their mark in politics, and by 1968 they could be expected to rise to further prominence as national politicians. Brother Bobby, a member of the Cabinet as Attorney General, also functioned as his closest adviser on government and political matters. Brother Teddy had to wait until 1962 before he could meet the Constitution's requirement that a U.S. Senator must be at least thirty years old. But he ran that year, and he won easily, even though he was only three years out of law school. In the Senate he gained seats on important committees.

In October, 1963, at the request of the President, Governor John Connally of Texas came to the White House to arrange a trip to his state by Kennedy. When Adlai Stevenson, now the U.S. Ambassador to the UN, learned of Kennedy's proposed trip, he expressed concern for the pressed concern for the President's safety. Only a month earlier, when Stevenson had gone to Dallas, political extremists had hit him on the head with a sign and spat on him. Several other persons, in addition to Stevenson, warned against the Presidential trip. Senator J. William Fulbright, chairman of the Senate Foreign Relations Committee, pleaded with Kennedy to avoid Dallas because of lurking assassins.

However, Kennedy scoffed at such fears, and on Thursday, November 21, he set his departure time at 11 A.M. that day for the flight to San Antonio and the beginning of his visit to Texas. His physician declared him in the best physical condition since his two operations in 1954 and 1955, even though he still had to wear a back brace and a metal lift in his left shoe, because that leg was three-quarters of an inch shorter than the other.

After kissing Caroline and John good-bye, Kennedy and his wife boarded Air Force One, the Presidential jet, on schedule for the three-and-a-half-hour flight to San Antonio. The entire city appeared to have turned out to greet the Kennedys, and the cheering never stopped until they left for Houston, where the President was scheduled to speak that evening at the Houston Coliseum. Afterward the Kennedys went on to Fort Worth to sleep. Then, shortly after noon the next day, Friday, November 22, they made a thirteen-minute flight to Love Field in Dallas. The size and warmth of the crowd at the airport delighted Kennedy, and once the motorcade began to wind its slow way along Dallas streets, the enthusiasm of the sidewalk crowds for the President and his lady was equally immense.

The destination was the Trade Mart, where Kennedy was scheduled to arrive at 1:35 P.M. for lunch and a speech. At 1:30, the long limousine carrying the Kennedys and Governor John Connally and his wife reached the corner of Elm and Houston.

"You certainly can't say that the people of Dallas haven't given you a warm welcome," Nellie Connally called to Kennedy in the seat behind her husband.

As the car headed toward a triple underpass, with an ugly building called the Texas School Book Depository on the right side, the President saw a small boy waving to him, and he raised his hand to wave back.

Suddenly rifle shots rang out . . .

# 4 Robert Francis Kennedy

ATTORNEY GENERAL Robert Kennedy was discussing Justice Department business at the side of his swimming pool at Hickory Hills, his McLean, Virginia, home, on November 22, 1963, when FBI Director J. Edgar Hoover telephoned him to report the assassination of his brother in Dallas. Kennedy's state of shock was so deep, said friends, that it lasted for months afterward.

In the political life of the United States, no two brothers were as devoted to each other as Jack and Bobby Kennedy. Yet not until Bobby reached adulthood was there an indication of the close relationship that eventually developed. In fact, Jack once confessed he was almost into his teens before he even became aware of Bobby's existence. He was twelve, he said, "the first time I met Bobby Kennedy. Of course, I had known him for three and a half years. After all, he was my brother."

It was the wide gulf of their age difference that had prevented an earlier friendship. But there were other reasons as well—differences in interests and personalities. "They didn't become really close until 1952," said their sister Eunice. "And it was politics that brought them together. Jack needed someone he could trust, someone who had loyalty to him. Jack knew he had a person like that with Bobby around."

When Robert Kennedy was born in his mother's bedroom in the family home in Brookline, Massachusetts, on November 20, 1925, he was the seventh of Rose and Joseph Kennedy's nine children. After Joe, Jr., and Jack had come four girls and then Bobby. "He was the smallest and thinnest, and we feared he might grow up puny and girlish," said his mother. "We soon realized there was no fear of that."

Since the girls were closer to him in age than his brothers, it was natural that they should become his playmates and competitors. This served to bring on a tremendous effort on his part to show his manliness. One way he did this was to insist on wearing sailor and soldier uniforms at every opportunity. A family friend recalled that when he returned home from church, he would tear off his clothes and jump into a uniform. Another way he believed he was showing masculinity was to misbehave and act mischievously. Mrs. Kennedy later said that he was the child who received the most spankings from her. Still another way was to pretend that injuries were not painful. One time when Bobby was playing in the tool shed, he broke a toe by accidentally dropping a radiator on his foot. In great agony, he returned to the house and said nothing for an hour about his pain. Finally, his mother saw from his expression that he was not well and rushed him to a doctor for treatment.

Whenever his sisters lost to him at any game, they were known to weep bitterly. And when Bobby lost to them, he felt the shame of a boy bested by girls. It was his belief that girls should not play jokes on boys, though he sometimes suffered as a result. On one occasion, his sister Eunice, four years his senior, threw some chocolate frosting at him. In man-sized anger he chased her through the Kennedy mansion and finally cornered her in front of a large table. Like a bull in the arena, he lowered his head and charged. But at the last moment she jumped aside, and he split his head open on the table.

His older brothers were almost of another generation. Though Jack ignored him, Joe took a patient, fatherly approach to Bobby. On their Bronxville, New York, estate, where Bobby spent most of his youth, Joe taught him to skate, to ride a bicycle, and to catch a football and baseball. As a youngster Bobby had poor coordination, a serious drawback in his desire to be an excellent athlete like Joe. "I dropped everything. I always fell down," he once admitted. "I always bumped my nose or my head."

For reasons unknown, Joe taught Bobby the rudiments of sailing, yet failed to teach him to swim. Jack recalled that shortly after he "met" Bobby, he was astounded by the antics of his four-year-old brother. Jack and Bobby were aboard a yawl off their summer home in Hyannis Port, far out in Nantucket Sound, when Bobby leaped over the side. When he came to the surface of the water, he thrashed his arms in a desperate effort to get back to the boat. Again and again he threw himself overboard and barely reached the yawl each time. Jack, who was eyeing him curiously, commented afterward that it showed "either a lot of guts or no sense at all, depending on how you looked at it."

With Joseph Kennedy, Sr., busy in Hollywood or on his financial schemes, Joe, Jr., was a father substitute, as well as a big brother, to the other youngsters with the exception of Jack. With Bobby close to Joe's side, there was always weekend excitement. A family friend noted that "they'd go up to Armonk to look at the animals at their farm, or horseback riding in Central Park. They were always outside, especially when it was snowing. Or they'd go upstate skiing."

When the elder Kennedy ended his movie-producing career in 1929, and before he went to work in the Roosevelt administration in 1934, he had ample opportunity to be with his children. His conclusion was that Bobby was more like him than any of the others. Bobby had his drive and frankness, as well as his tendency to be moved easily by his emotions.

Bobby was also the first Kennedy child to reveal an interest in earning money. While Joe and Jack kept after their father with pleas that he increase their small allowances, Bobby bred rabbits and sold them to rich youngsters in the Bronxville mansion area. Unwilling to spend his profits, he opened his own savings account at a nearby bank.

For a time he was also a door-to-door magazine salesman, selling single copies and taking subscriptions for the *Saturday Evening Post*. At first he delivered copies by bicycle. But when he found this tiresome, his father's chauffeur drove him from house to house in the family's

Rolls-Royce. After a few months he stayed home, and the chauffeur was obliged to make the deliveries. Even this method ended, and the magazines collected in high piles in Bobby's room until one of the many maids reported it to Mrs. Kennedy. She quickly ended the business.

One of the several reasons for the closeness between Bobby and his mother was that he was an extremely religious boy. When he was seven in 1933, he received his first communion. He took great pleasure in serving as an altar boy and never forgot the duties. In fact, when he was almost forty and found an altar boy missing at church in Hyannis Port, he took the absent boy's place and performed his functions without error. This deep religious bent led him to consider becoming a priest. But when the time actually came to decide on a career, he chose law.

Like his older brothers, Bobby was early attracted to politics. "As far back as I can remember," he once wrote, "politics was taken with special fervor and relish in our house. . . . I can hardly remember a mealtime when the conversation was not dominated by what Franklin D. Roosevelt was doing or what was happening round the world."

From Washington, where his father was working as chairman of the Securities and Exchange Commission, came a letter from President Roosevelt to Bobby that made the youngster gasp. The contents revealed that the busy President had taken time off from his enormous duties to discuss Bobby with the elder Kennedy. The letter, dated July 12, 1935, read in part: "Your Dad has told me that you are a stamp collector and I thought you might like to have these stamps to add to your collection."

Bobby's formal education began in the public schools in Bronxville, and a principal later recalled the impression he made as a ten-year-old boy in the fifth grade: "He was a nice freckle-faced little kid, his hair some shade of brown, a regular boy. He needed no special handling. It seemed hard for him to finish his work sometimes, but he was only ten after all."

Like his brother Jack and unlike Joe, Bobby was an indifferent student. Joe could cram the study of an entire course into the night before an examination and get a top grade. Had Jack or Bobby tried this, each would have failed. These two could get good grades only if they studied methodically day after day. Unfortunately, Jack and Bobby were too interested in sports to make this effort. In addition, in his youth Bobby had little patience for sitting still long enough to go through any book. "Bobby didn't read much when he was young," said Rose Kennedy. "He was one of those I had to keep urging to read."

Soon after Bobby entered the exclusive Riverdale Country School, which brothers Joe and Jack had attended earlier, Joseph Kennedy was appointed American Ambassador to Great Britain in the spring of 1938. It meant that all the children except Joe and Jack, who were going to Harvard, moved to London with their parents.

There Bobby and younger brother Teddy, who was born in 1932, were sent to the Gibbs School, a Protestant prep school. Eunice, Patricia, and Jean attended Catholic schools. Oldest sister Rosemary, who was mentally retarded, was kept at her mother's side, and eighteen-year-old Kick became her mother's assistant embassy hostess. Life in England did not agree with Bobby. He found the national sport of cricket dull compared with football and baseball, and he was not pleased to be forced to play the game at Gibbs. "I think he loathed his school," said an English friend of Jack's, who met Bobby at that time. Being forced to wear the school's bell-shaped hat infuriated him. In addition, Gibbs enforced compulsory chapel with a Protestant service, and Bobby refused to attend. At one point he packed his belongings and showed up at the American Embassy to announce to his father that he was through with the school. He was ordered back, of course.

While in England, Bobby wanted to join the Boy Scouts until he learned he would have to swear allegiance to the king. At first his father made a time-consuming effort to have him accepted without this condition. When he failed, Bobby's pleas led him to write to the Boy Scout headquarters in New York, and his son was finally enrolled as an absentee member of an American troop.

On September 1, 1939, when the Germans invaded Poland, Bobby's stay in England began drawing to a close.

Once she had her children home safely in Bronxville, Mrs. Kennedy listened to Bobby's request that he be sent to a Catholic prep school. The school year had already begun, and she acted hastily in enrolling him at St. Paul's Academy in Concord, the capital of New Hampshire. One of the boys at the school was John V. Lindsay, later mayor of New York. Bobby was hardly gone when he wrote his mother that St. Paul's was a Protestant and not a Catholic school.

This time she checked carefully before transferring him to the Portsmouth Priory School in Rhode Island. The priory belonged to the Order of St. Benedict, and a large group of Benedictine monks had their monastery on the school grounds. From the daily school schedule at the priory, Mrs. Kennedy readily saw that religion was heavily emphasized. Bobby and the other boys attended mass daily at 6:35 A.M., then had morning prayers at 7 A.M., chapel at 6 P.M., and confessions after dinner. The boys also sang the Sunday morning high mass with the Benedictine monks, as well as the Sunday evening prayers.

The priory was to Bobby's liking. But word of his school choice soon reached his father. Despite the ambassador's growing trouble with President Roosevelt, the elder Kennedy forgot his problems long enough to order his son's immediate removal from the priory to a nonsectarian prep school.

This time Bobby landed at Milton Academy, outside Boston, where rich youths were prepared for Ivy League colleges. Having been brought up in a family that depended on itself for companionship and entertainment, Bobby's natural shyness and lack of experience made it difficult for him to acquire friends at the new school. In fact, David Hackett, a boy also interested in sports, became his sole friend at Milton. Other students there found Bobby either silent or too vigorous in expressing his opinions. "He was no good at small talk; he was no good at social amenities," one Milton student later recalled. The dean went further in describing Bobby: "He wouldn't be a fellow you'd pick out of his class, as he did not win the poll for 'Most Likely to Succeed.' He was not a naturally brilliant student, who just kicked off the grades. He had to work, and he always worked hard. I remember him mostly on the football field. You knew he was around. He was pretty active—he'd win at anything."

Like most of his fellow students at Milton, Bobby found it difficult to concentrate on his studies because World War II was in full eruption around the globe. Brother Joe was in England flying on naval patrol duty and Jack was recuperating from his PT-109 disaster when Bobby decided he could no longer continue civilian life. So in October, 1943, when he was only seventeen and at the start of his senior year at Milton, he enlisted in the U.S. Naval Reserve. The following March, when he was sent to the officers training school at Harvard, the authorities at Milton agreed to record him as a high school graduate.

Bobby was visiting his family at Hyannis Port the first weekend in August, 1944, and he was present as his grief-stricken father broke the news of Joe's death in the explosion of his plane. Word of this tragedy so stunned Bobby that he asked to get out of the officers training program and be sent to sea. But his orders, instead, were to report to Bates College in Lewiston, Maine, for special college course work.

There he remained from November, 1944, to July, 1945, before reporting back to the Navy's training unit for officers at Harvard. His time spent in classrooms gave him sufficient credits to be listed as a Harvard sophomore, but Bobby was too uneasy to continue courses. The war was already over in Europe, the Pacific fighting was fast reaching a climax, and he wanted to get into the war to avenge Joe's death.

One day that summer he went to Washington to see Secretary of the Navy James V. Forrestal, a friend of his father's. Forrestal was making last-minute preparations for his trip to the Potsdam Conference with President Truman, but he listened patiently to the young man's demand to see action. When Forrestal pointed out that he would have to quit officers training school and become a lowly second-class seaman, Bobby quickly announced his willingness.

A new 2,200-ton destroyer, the USS *Joseph P. Kennedy, Jr.,* had just been launched, and Bobby was to serve aboard her. However, Bobby's elation in obtaining sea duty gave way to dismay a short time later. The *Joseph P. Kennedy, Jr.* was ordered into Caribbean waters, instead of the Pacific, and Bobby spent several months performing the usual menial chores of the second-class seaman until his discharge from the Navy on May 30, 1946.

Hardly was he back in Hyannis Port and out of his bell-bottom trousers and into civilian clothes when his father put him to work. His brother Jack was running in the June, 1946, Democratic primary for his party's nomination as its candidate for a seat in the U.S. House of Representatives. Dozens of Jack's service and school friends had come to Boston to work in his campaign, professional politicians were working on strategy, and the Kennedy females were joining in the staging of teas and receptions.

Mike Neville, the former mayor of Cambridge, was

the favorite among the ten Democrats running for the nomination in the Eleventh District, and Joseph Kennedy turned to twenty-year-old Bobby to help deflate Neville in his home territory. In parceling out campaign zones, the elder Kennedy assigned the seamy area of East Cambridge to Bobby and told him that the experts expected Neville to win there by five to one over his combined opponents. If Bobby could cut this down to four to one, said his father, this would be of immense help to Jack.

When he set up his headquarters in this poor Italian section, Bobby followed the usual campaign course of ringing doorbells and getting himself invited to spaghetti dinners. But he appeared to be making little headway in promoting his brother until one day when he looked out of his headquarters window and saw boys playing softball in the park across the street. He was outside in an instant and dashing across the avenue. He forgot the campaign in spending the afternoon playing ball. However, word soon spread throughout the neighborhood that the young millionaire Irishman did not think he was too high-class for the people living there, and his campaign lapse became his brother's gain. On election night, after the votes were in, the elder Kennedy and Jack were pleased to find that half the East Cambridge vote was for John F. Kennedy. This added a great deal to his smashing victory over his Democratic opponents.

Since the Republicans were weak in the Eleventh Congressional District and victory for the Democratic nominee was a certainty in the November general election, Bobby withdrew from politics immediately following the primary. But to celebrate his successful effort, his father sent him and Jack's Choate roommate, Lem Billings, on a tour of South America.

The two traveled as far as Argentina, and Bobby returned home with stories about the deep poverty he had seen in each country. This awakening concern with the plight of the very poor was fortified soon after he arrived back at Hyannis Port. He took a job for the rest of the summer at the Columbia Trust Company, where his father had been president at the age of twenty-five. His assignment turned out to be that of a rent collector on slum properties Columbia Trust owned in East Boston. Daily he saw the inside of tenement hovels populated by miserable adults and swarms of children, and what he saw shocked him.

It was with relief that the fall of 1946 came and he could return to Harvard to begin his sophomore year. He focused his attention on athletics now. Although he weighed less than 150 pounds, he went out for football and made the squad. Kenny O'Donnell, captain of the Crimson eleven, said, "I can't think of anyone who had less right to make the varsity squad than Bobby, when he first came out for practice. The war was over and we had plenty of manpower, all of it bigger, faster and more experienced than he. But every afternoon he would be down on the field an hour early and he always stayed an hour later. He just made himself better by maximizing his abilities."

Harvard awarded football letters only to those who played against Yale, its traditional rival. In his three years on the Harvard team, brother Joe had somehow failed to play against "Old Eli," and as a result, he had never won the coveted crimson *H*. Bobby did not get into the Yale game in 1946, and in 1947 an accident seemed certain to deprive him of winning his letter: In football practice, Bobby had run out from his end position and collided with an equipment truck.

The accident had left him with a broken right leg, and on the Saturday of the Yale game he sat forlornly on the bench with his fractured leg bound in a plaster cast. Late-afternoon shadows were falling while Yale built a commanding lead of 31 to 14. Harvard finally made another touchdown, and the score changed to 31 to 21. The referee said time remained for only a single play—the Harvard kickoff to Yale.

Suddenly the voice of Harvard coach Richard Harlow came down the bench. "Kennedy, go in!" Bobby hobbled onto the field and took his place just before the kickoff ball sailed end over end to a Yale receiver. In a moment the Yale man came charging down the field, eluding one tackle after another until Bobby brought him down. For his few seconds of action, Bobby had won his *H*.

Like Joe and Jack before him, Bobby lived at Winthrop House in the Harvard Yard. However, unlike his brothers, Bobby's acquaintances tended to be students whose families struggled to pay their way through Harvard. Those who learned that Bobby came from a wealthy family had difficulty in reconciling the fact with this bushy-haired, long-toothed young fellow in wrinkled clothes. One of Bobby's friends said that on his twenty-first birthday Bobby showed him a check for $1,000 that his father had given him for not smoking or drinking. "When I looked at it, I almost fainted," said the friend.

On invitation, Bobby was a member of the fairly exclusive Spee Club and the Hasty Pudding Institute of

1770. But he did not participate in social affairs as many other rich young men did. Asked why, he replied, "Nobody who ever went to them made any real contribution. What's the good of going to those things and drinking? I'd rather do something else."

The "something else" was to spend hour after hour in conversation or in listening silently to others. "I didn't go to class very much," he admitted. "I used to talk and argue a lot, mostly about sports and politics. I began thinking about issues about the time I went to college." Those who knew him best said he was "very shy—not at all pushy." One young man remembered, "Sometimes we would have very heated discussions on politics, and at the end he would ask about somebody, 'Do you think I hurt his feelings?'"

In early 1948 Bobby discovered that he had sufficient credits to be graduated in June with a major in government after only two full years at Harvard. Although school authorities agreed that this was true, his elation ended when his application to Harvard Law School was rejected. Bobby then applied successfully to the University of Virginia Law School in March. On his form he wrote: "I am about to leave on a six-month tour of the Middle East and Europe."

This was not idle talk. The United Nations had partitioned Palestine into independent Jewish and Arab nations, and in May, 1948, when the United States and the Soviet Union recognized Israel, her Arab neighbors immediately went to war with the new nation. Bobby had planned a sight-seeing trip into the area, but when war broke out, he asked his father to help him land a newspaper job as a foreign correspondent. This was a simple matter for the elder Kennedy, who admired his son's desire for action. A call to the publisher of the Boston *Post,* and Bobby was quickly on his way to the Middle East.

Soon the byline of Robert Kennedy began appearing in the *Post.* He went into the battle areas, observed the strength of the antagonists, gauged their will to fight, as well as their training, and reported that the Israelis had "much more spirit and discipline and determination" than the Arabs. "They are a young, tough, determined nation," he told *Post* readers in one dispatch. "They fight with unparalleled courage. This is their greatest and last chance; there will be no turning back."

The sense of constant danger did not frighten him. Once he wanted to go to Jerusalem from Tel Aviv. He found a convoy leader who offered him a seat in a truck, but shortly before the convoy pulled out, a tank commander told him he could travel in a tank. The latter choice pleased Bobby more, and he went to Jerusalem in this fashion. On arrival, he learned that the convoy had been wiped out en route.

When the war receded into a cease-fire, Bobby went to West Berlin, also a major international problem that summer. Stalin had barred highway access to West Berlin from American and British occupation zones in conquered Germany in an effort to force the Western allies to give up their hold on West Berlin. While several of his military advisers called for war with the USSR, President Truman instead started a Berlin airlift to supply the needs of the people of West Berlin by airplanes until Stalin called off his scheme.

After covering the operation of the airlift for the *Post,* enterprising young Kennedy made plans to visit behind the Iron Curtain and observe the Communist governments of Eastern Europe. However, his plans came to naught, and his visa was not honored. The charge of the Hungarian government was that he was the personal spy of Francis Cardinal Spellman, the Archbishop of New York.

By September, 1948, Bobby's days as a foreign correspondent were behind him. When he appeared in Charlottesville, Virginia, to become a law school freshman, he was still shy and quiet. When he did speak, he tended to be too frank. And he continued to live like a person with meager funds. A classmate recalled that he "had a 1941 automobile. It was sort of falling apart." The place where he chose to live was a small wooden cottage in a field close to the railroad tracks, the former dwelling of a tenant worker on a farm. He shared expenses with George Tierney, a fellow law student, and the two were kept awake on rainy nights by the pounding of raindrops on the tin roof. A burned-oil odor filled the small rooms in wintertime since the cottage was heated by an old oil stove.

Bobby studied as little as he had at Harvard. One professor labeled him "no bookworm"; others said he contributed little to classroom discussions. Required to take a course on how to use the law library, he refused to attend classes or do the assignments on the ground that the course was an insult to postgraduate college students. As a result, his grade was an F. Outside of decent grades in labor law and American constitutional law, he was only an average student according to his grades. He was graduated in the middle of his class scholastically, standing fifty-sixth out of 124.

Much of Bobby's time at the University of Virginia was devoted to the Law School Forum, a student organization that invited speakers to the campus. When Bobby came to Charlottesville, the forum existed in name only. But after he won election as its president, he undertook to invite national figures to the campus.

Chief credit for the caliber of the speakers belonged to Joseph Kennedy, who enlisted the services of many important friends. Among those who took time off from their duties to travel to Charlottesville were Supreme Court Justice William O. Douglas, former government trustbuster Thurman Arnold, Jack Kennedy, and Senator Joseph McCarthy. Joseph Kennedy also came to Charlottesville as a forum speaker, and his speech gained national attention in the press. The Korean War had begun in June, 1950, a few months earlier, and in the midst of heavy fighting there the elder Kennedy had called for the withdrawal of American military forces from that Asian peninsula.

The forum series produced moments of humor and emotional stress. One funny experience involved Senator McCarthy, who was already in the limelight with his accusations of widespread Communist membership among government workers. McCarthy was afraid of dogs. While he was in the midst of thunderous threats against federal employees, a dog wandered into the hall and walked up the aisle toward him. Suddenly McCarthy broke off his speech and screamed in terror, "Get that dog out of here!" The hound was removed, but so was the image of the Senator as an unflinching fighter.

Bobby personally gained newspaper coverage across the country when he invited Ralph Bunche, an American

Negro and high UN official, to speak at the forum. After Bunche accepted, the university's board of visitors told Bobby that state law barred the mixing of races in public gatherings. Instead of informing Bunche that the invitation was withdrawn, Bobby told reporters about the situation, and newspapers quickly gave front-page coverage to the controversy, playing up Bobby as a student who would not give in to college authorities. Finally, to end the squabble, the university president sanctioned the appearance of Bunche, who spoke without incident.

Certainly the major event during Bobby's three years at law school was his marriage to Ethel Skakel in June, 1950. Ethel, a devout Catholic whose father owned the large Great Lakes Carbon Corporation, was a roommate of Bobby's younger sister Jean at Manhattanville College of the Sacred Heart in New York. Two years Bobby's junior, she was seventeen in 1944 when she met the young naval officer trainee at a ski lodge at Mont Tremblant, a popular winter spot in Canada.

Unfortunately, her sister Pat was also there, and Bobby fell in love with her. While Ethel pined in silence, Pat and Bobby went together for two years. Then, in 1946, when Bobby took over the East Cambridge area in his brother Jack's primary campaign for the House, Ethel came to Boston and also worked in that campaign as a doorbell ringer. Bobby saw her several times in this period. When the primary ended, he had fallen out of love with Pat and into love with Ethel. If Bobby's parents ever held doubts about their future daughter-in-law, these were ended when they learned that her senior year's thesis was on Jack's book *Why England Slept*.

To his parents she seemed just the person to complement Bobby's shy and serious personality. Her college class annual of 1949 called her "one minute a picture of mischief and the next alive with mischief." Like Bobby, she was interested in sports; she was a hockey teacher at one time. In August, 1948, he had taken time off as a foreign correspondent to join her at Wembley, England, where the Olympic Games were then in progress.

So Joseph and Rose Kennedy were especially pleased when Bobby told them he planned to marry Ethel. Jack served as Bobby's best man, and the New York *Times* in describing the wedding at Greenwich, Connecticut, Ethel's residence, wrote: "In a garden setting of white peonies, lilies and dogwood in St. Mary's Roman Catholic Church here this morning. . . ."

In his final year at law school, Bobby moved from the little cottage and rented a large white house adjoining the campus for himself and his bride. Graduation came in June, 1951, just weeks before the birth of their first child, Kathleen Hartington, named after Bobby's oldest sister, Kick, who had been killed in May, 1948, when her plane crashed into a European mountaintop. At the time of Kathleen's birth, Bobby was an admirer of Senator Joseph McCarthy, and the Senator became his daughter's godfather.

Kathleen was a few months old when Jack Kennedy offered to help Bobby celebrate fatherhood and his recent law degree by taking him on a trip around the world. Jack's primary purpose in this long tour was to be able to campaign for the Senate the following year as a man who had firsthand experience with the world's trouble spots.

**149**

The trip also served to change his big-brother relationship toward Bobby, though toward the close of their travels another Kennedy tragedy almost occurred. They were in the Far East when Jack's back began paining him; then an attack of malaria came. With his temperature rising above 106 degrees, he was flown to a military hospital in Okinawa. "They didn't think he would live," Bobby later described the concern of physicians. But after a few days the temperature dropped to normal, the back pain ebbed, and they returned to the United States without further mishap.

Bobby had no doubts about what he wanted to do upon becoming a lawyer. For years his father had dominated dinner conversation with his theme that a life devoted to public service was the most satisfying way to spend one's adult years. As a result, said Bobby, "I wanted to go into the government, and looked to it as an opportunity for an exciting life."

Bobby's first job in public service was as a $4,200-a-year beginning lawyer with the Internal Security Division of the Justice Department. This division examined evidence pertaining to Americans accused of serving as spies for the Soviet Union. Bobby found the work fascinating, but he had hardly grown accustomed to keeping regular office hours when he was transferred to the Criminal Division's branch in Brooklyn.

There, as one of dozens of young lawyers in the office of the U.S. Attorney for New York, he was assigned to equally interesting work. Instead of spies, the object of his investigation was corrupt government officials. Within a few months, he prepared court cases involving two top officials of the Internal Revenue Service who had cheated on their income taxes.

Other cases were assigned to him, but he had not yet begun to collect court evidence for government prosecutors when his father phoned him to quit his job and come to Boston. Jack Kennedy's 1952 campaign for the U.S. Senate against Republican Senator Henry Cabot Lodge was limping along, said the elder Kennedy, and Bobby was needed to help his brother.

In 1946, when Jack had run for the House the first time, Joseph Kennedy had employed Mark Dalton, a young lawyer and politician, as his son's campaign manager. Dalton had continued to serve in this post during Jack's next two campaigns for the House and for his Senate try. However, as the 1952 campaign began to develop, Joseph Kennedy grew concerned that not enough effort was being put forth in his son's behalf. One day, in a fit of nervous tension and anger, he scolded Dalton, who quit the next morning. The call to Bobby at the Brooklyn Federal Building was a demand that he return home and replace Dalton as campaign manager.

"Bobby didn't want to work in the campaign of 1952," said one of his friends. "He preferred staying in the Justice Department." But family loyalty was the overriding consideration, and he resigned as a government lawyer.

Animosity was commonplace among old Democratic politicians in Massachusetts when baby-faced twenty-six-year-old Bobby showed up at Kennedy campaign headquarters at 122 Bowdoin Street in Boston. This was a poorly furnished apartment that Jack rented and maintained to serve as his "permanent" address in his home state. "What had Bobby done up to that time politically? Nothing!" one politician complained. "Not a thing and all of a sudden he was there as campaign manager, waving the banners."

Another Bay State politician sauntered into Kennedy headquarters one afternoon and expressed his hurt feelings when Bobby failed to greet him by name. "You're asking me who I am?" he yelled at the young man. "You mean nobody here knows me? And you call this a political headquarters?" Bobby ordered him to leave and not to return.

Still another time, said Jack Kennedy, "I remember in my 1952 campaign when some politicians came into our headquarters and stood around gabbing. Finally, Bobby told them, 'Here are some envelopes. You want to address them, fine. Otherwise, wait outside.' They addressed the envelopes."

There was one politician who would not take orders from Bobby. He was Governor Paul Dever, who was running for reelection on the same ticket with Jack. One day Bobby stormed into the governor's office and began scolding him for saying things in his speeches that differed from what Jack was saying.

The governor opened the door and waved Bobby outside. Then he phoned Joseph Kennedy and in anger shouted, "I know you're an important man around here and all that. But I'm telling you this and I mean it. Keep that fresh kid of yours out of my sight from here on in."

There was more to Bobby's role in that election than antagonizing other politicians. One task was to organize speakers in his brother's behalf, and although he was personally frightened at the prospect of standing before an audience, he had apt suggestions for others. Obliged to speak at a rally, he delivered the shortest address of the campaign: "My brother Jack couldn't be here," he said. "My mother couldn't be here. My sister Eunice couldn't be here. My sister Pat couldn't be here. My sister Jean couldn't be here. But if my brother Jack were here, he'd tell you that Lodge has a very bad voting record. Thank you."

Bobby's chief function when he came to Boston in June, 1952, was to serve as the organizer of campaign workers, who in turn were expected to bring out the vote for Jack. "We were in a tough fight," said his older brother. "It was essential that we set up our own organization in every community across the state. My first campaign manager had had a pretty rough time trying to do this. Then Bobby came in and did the job in three weeks."

Bobby's technique was to organize the 286 "secretaries" in the cities and towns across the state to direct the local Kennedy forces. This method was selected so that the local chieftains would be personally loyal to Kennedy as their candidate, not to Kennedy as part of the state Democratic organization. "We tried to organize every town of over six hundred votes" was how Bobby later explained his handiwork.

However, even while he was establishing the Kennedy organization, he conceived of an important breakthrough in acquiring votes for his brother. One day, while glancing over the list of registered Democratic voters in a town, he was surprised by the small number on the rolls. He knew that the police department had address listings of every resident in town, and when he checked the police lists against the voting registration list in a section of town known to be heavily Democratic, he found few Democrats there were registered.

This led him to order his "secretaries" to make similar tests of their communities. The results were the same as those he had found and led to a large-scale effort to get Democrats to register so that they could vote. The success of this scheme was enormous: A hundred thousand Democrats registered to vote for the first time. This was 30,000 votes more than the 70,000 majority by which Jack Kennedy defeated Lodge.

Of course, the Kennedy victory cannot be attributed entirely to this plan of Bobby's, for there is some uncertainty regarding the number of registered Democrats who voted for Lodge once they entered the polling booths. One reason was offered by a lieutenant of Lodge's, who was a Protestant, for Kennedy's victory in heavily Roman Catholic Massachusetts. Ethel Kennedy had given birth to her second child, Joseph Patrick Kennedy, on September 24, 1952. Said the Lodge aide: "When Archbishop Cushing baptized that baby in a special weekday ceremony just before the election, that cut the heart right out from us."

After he had won his Senate seat, Jack Kennedy commented on the charges of politicians against his brother. "I don't pay any attention to the beefs," he said. "Every politician in Massachusetts was mad at Bobby after 1952, but we had the best organization in history. And what friend who was really worthwhile has he lost? I don't recall."

In January, 1953, Bobby took a controversial job when he went to work for his father's friend, Senator Joseph McCarthy. With the Republicans holding a majority in both houses of Congress, McCarthy was now in a position of power as chairman of the Senate Government Operations Committee and its Permanent Investigations Subcommittee. These assignments put the Wisconsin Senator in the driver's seat in investigating waste and fraud in government activities and subversion of federal employees. Great concern existed among champions of civil liberties that McCarthy planned to use his new authority to label additional thousands of Americans as "disloyal" without giving the accused a chance to defend themselves.

Later, when Senator Kennedy was asked to explain why he had not spoken out against McCarthyism, he said, "I was caught in a bad situation. My brother Bobby was working for Joe. I was against it. I didn't want him to work for Joe, but he wanted to. And how could I get up there and denounce Joe McCarthy when my own brother was working for him?" In addition, he explained, "I had never known the sort of people who were called before the McCarthy Committee. I agree that many of them were seriously manhandled, but they all represented a different world to me. What I mean is, I did not identify with them, and so I did not get as worked up as other liberals did."

Nor did Bobby at that time. Besides asking McCarthy to be daughter Kathleen's godfather, he viewed the Senator in 1953 as a man performing a necessary function. For example, his own opinion of President Franklin Roosevelt, as expressed in a law school paper he had written, was similar to the position held by his father and brother Jack—that Roosevelt had "sold out" the United States to the Communists at his 1945 conference with Stalin.

Bobby was one of fifteen assistant counsels employed by McCarthy. His first full-time assignment was to investigate trade between American allies in the Korean War and Red China, the ally of Communist North Korea. By checking shipping records, Bobby found that during the preceding year American allies had carried $2 billion worth of goods to Red China.

This was a sensational finding. While Bobby gained personal publicity in newspapers for his work, the Eisenhower administration denounced the study for undermining its own efforts to end that trade. Arthur Krock, the Kennedy family friend, praised Bobby's work in his New York *Times* column as "an example of Congressional investigation at its highest." Krock also noted that "though very young, he [Bobby] has already given the impression he is painstaking and accurate."

There were to be no further investigations by Bobby. McCarthy's chief counsel was Roy Cohn, a brilliant young attorney who could not get along with Bobby. The assistant counsel was forever attacking Cohn and David Schine, a subcommittee investigator, for operating on the basis of "preconceived" prejudices, not facts. "They were not going to let the facts interfere," Bobby once charged.

As a result, he told McCarthy he could not remain on the subcommittee staff with Cohn, and he resigned on July 31, 1953. McCarthy's letter of regret to him praised Bobby for having done "a tremendous job" in only six months.

*Robert Francis Kennedy*

After he left the McCarthy Subcommittee, Bobby considered entering private law practice. But at the time his father was a member of the second Hoover Commission, a Presidential commission studying ways to eliminate duplication and waste in the Executive Branch of the government. When the elder Kennedy prevailed on former President Herbert Hoover to name Bobby a commission counsel, he forgot about private practice.

In the Hoover Commission's work, several task forces had been established to delve into various federal functions. Bobby's assigned job was to work with the findings of the task forces and help write their reports. However, the task forces had not yet done their work when he joined the commission, and after sitting about restlessly waiting for them, he quit in February, 1954. When he did, Hoover expressed his regret at the young man's impatience. "I am sorry to hear that you are leaving us," the former President wrote Bobby. "I realize, however, that there is little work to do until the task forces have reported and that a restless soul like you wants to work."

Only days after he left his father and Hoover, Bobby returned to the McCarthy Permanent Subcommittee on Investigations. The previous July the three Democratic Senators on the subcommittee had resigned because of the dictatorial manner in which McCarthy ran its business. Then, early in 1954, they had taken their subcommittee seats again, after McCarthy had agreed to let them select a minority party counsel to serve them. Senator John McClellan, a friend of Joseph Kennedy's and the ranking Democrat on the subcommittee, appointed Bobby to this post.

It was as minority counsel that Bobby took part in the

1954 hearings that ruined McCarthy. The Wisconsin Senator had begun a hearing to show that the generals at Camp Kilmer, New Jersey, had acted in a pro-Communist manner. When the Eisenhower administration decided to fight this attack on the U.S. Army, TV networks gave thirty-six days of attention to what became known as the Army-McCarthy Hearings.

During much of the hearings, Bobby was visible on TV, sitting behind the three Democratic Senators and advising them on questions to ask McCarthy and other witnesses. On occasion, Bobby asked questions, and once he and Roy Cohn had a heated exchange, with Cohn the angry loser by a wide margin. Afterward, when Bobby was leaving the room, Cohn yelled, "Do you want to fight?" Bobby ignored him.

As a result of the hearings, McCarthy's undemocratic methods lay fully exposed to a national audience. This induced the Senate to appoint a special committee to try him for misconduct. Four months later, on December 2, 1954, the Senate censured McCarthy for his disrespect of the upper chamber by a vote of 67 to 22.

This broke McCarthy's spirit. His health declined along with his dwindling reputation, and he died in 1957. "I liked him," Bobby said later, "and yet he was so heavy-handed. He was sensitive and yet insensitive. He would get a guilty feeling after he blasted somebody. He didn't anticipate the results of what he was doing."

When the Democrats won control of Congress in the 1954 elections, Senator McClellan replaced McCarthy as chairman, and Bobby became chief counsel of the subcommittee. As head of a large staff of lawyers and investigators, many of whom were almost twice his age, Bobby was frequently in the news as an example of a young man with an important job. "Lots of young lawyers could handle a job like mine if people would stop thinking of thirty-five as the minimum age of real responsibility," he said after the Junior Chamber of Commerce selected him in 1955 as one of the nation's "Ten Outstanding Young Men."

In his early years as chief counsel, Bobby twice expanded his political horizons in other areas. The first occasion came after Congress adjourned in August, 1955, when he went abroad to study the internal affairs of the Soviet Union. "It was his father's idea that Bobby should go to Russia, and he asked me to take him," said Supreme Court Justice William Douglas, once the elder Kennedy's employee. "Joe used to keep each member of the family on an escalator. The trip took seven weeks. Bobby didn't talk much, but he was very observant.

"The trip to Russia shook him up. We are brought up in a closed society which thinks that everything Communist is evil. But in Siberia he got sick—he had a temperature of 105 degrees—and a Russian lady doctor sat for thirty-six hours by his bed without leaving and saved his life. He was unconscious (probably suffering from pneumonia). He lost seventeen pounds and looked like a ghost."

Bobby was also shaken by a second experience. After Adlai Stevenson won his second nomination for the Presidency, Bobby, who had taken time off from his job to help his brother win the Vice Presidential nomination, worked through an entire night in vain to swing convention delegates behind Jack. When Senator Estes Kefauver of Tennessee won, Bobby analyzed the reasons and

159

passed along priceless information to Jack for use in 1960. "It really struck me that it wasn't the issues that mattered. It was the friendships," he concluded. "So many people said to me they would rather vote for Jack, but they were going to vote for Estes Kefauver because he had sent them a card or gone to their home. So I said right there that we should forget the issues and send Christmas cards and go to their homes next time."

Bobby gained further experience of great importance to Jack when he spent the rest of the summer and fall as assistant to Stevenson's campaign manager. Because of his youth and his status as an outsider, he was treated as though he were not present. "Nobody asked me anything; nobody wanted me to do anything; nobody consulted me," he admitted. But this was to his brother's future advantage, for, he added, "I had time to watch everything —I filled complete notebooks with notes on how a Presidential campaign should be run. Or rather, I was learning what not to do."

These "what not to do" items included going unbriefed on the local leading Democrats when traveling on the campaign trail; having the candidate become too weary, use words of many syllables, and speak too long; and running a stingy campaign.

Following Eisenhower's second victory over Stevenson, Bobby returned to his committee work in January, 1957. This time he was to concentrate on investigating labor racketeering.

A reporter had told him about corruption among top officials of the Teamsters Union, the largest single labor organization in the world with a membership of almost 2,000,000. To check on the newsman's tip, Bobby flew to Seattle, registered at a hotel as Mr. Rogers, and questioned several persons regarding the activities of Dave Beck, the Teamsters president, who lived in that city. Then, convinced that there was sufficient cause for a full investigation, he spoke to Senator McClellan on his return. The Senator in turn induced the Senate to establish a Select Committee on Improper Activities of Labor and Management, with himself as chairman. Bobby became his staff director and boss of sixty-five employees.

The press shortened the title of the committee to the Labor Rackets Committee, and under this name it gained major headlines in the next three years as Bobby carried on legal warfare against the leaders of several unions. His investigators went through tons of financial records and letters, talked to thousands of persons, and gave Bobby the raw material for his cross-examinations of union officers and gangsters when they took the witness chair before the committee.

Although the committee examined the activities of several unions, Bobby concentrated most of his effort on the Teamsters. President Dave Beck, who refused to answer questions when called before the committee in the Senate Caucus Room, was later tried in court on evidence collected by Bobby. A jury found him guilty of income-tax evasion for using union funds for his own purposes.

Beck's successor as Teamsters president was James Riddle Hoffa, whom Bobby pursued relentlessly in his attempts to put him behind bars. In preparing evidence and committee questions for Hoffa, Bobby and his staff put in a 9 A.M. to 9 P.M. day seven days a week. To counter all this, said Hoffa, "I sat down and put on paper everything I could think of they might ask questions about.

Then I got with my lawyers and we went over every item. We'd rehearse what we thought Kennedy would do, and and we got it right near every time."

National TV audiences watched the two antagonists in fascination. To Bobby's carefully determined questions came Hoffa's unfrightened responses that he could not remember the incident involved. In a single day as a witness, Hoffa began 111 of his replies with "To the best of my recollection."

"This is a lawyer?" Hoffa openly scoffed at him. "You know how he got his job, don't you? . . . Nepotism." In turn, Bobby expressed surprise that Hoffa hated him personally. He wrote afterward that Hoffa stared at him "across the counsel table with a deep, strange, penetrating expression. It was the look of a man obsessed by his enmity, and it came particularly from his eyes . . . this stare of absolute evilness."

Many who watched their confrontations said that Bobby was persecuting Hoffa by his ceaseless effort to force him to admit wrongdoing. Some said he questioned Hoffa the way Simon Legree would a runaway slave. But one Washington lawyer commented that "far from browbeating Hoffa, it was more a case of Hoffa browbeating him."

Twice Bobby Kennedy's committee investigations led to indictments and court trials for Hoffa. But each time Hoffa won acquittal. One case involved Hoffa's alleged wiretapping. The second concerned alleged bribery.

In the latter instance, a man named Cye Chesty visited Bobby in private and told him that Hoffa had agreed to pay him $2,000 a month if he got a job on the committee and transmitted copies of anti-Hoffa material to him.

Bobby then put Chesty on his staff and gave him documents for Hoffa. The FBI was alerted and arrested Hoffa immediately after Chesty handed him some written material.

"If Hoffa isn't convicted I'll jump off the Capitol dome," said Bobby. A jury freed the Teamsters president, and his lawyer offered to send Bobby a parachute.

In September, 1959, when he quit his job with the Senate Labor Rackets Committee after almost three years of hard work, Bobby said frankly that he had not been successful. "In the months since the committee began to work," he concluded, "conditions in the labor and management fields have actually grown worse instead of better." Yet Bobby's remark ignored the fact that about fifteen unions and sixty companies had changed their practices for the better because of his investigations.

When Bobby left his committee work, his purpose was to help his brother again. Three years earlier, as he watched the Vice Presidential nomination go to Senator Kefauver, Jack had said, "I'm not running for Vice President any more. I'm now running for President."

His first move had come that fall during the second Stevenson-Eisenhower campaign, when he made 150 speeches. One purpose was to aid his party's ticket, but another was to meet local political leaders for the first time. After this, when Jack spent much of the next three years traveling the nation to meet more influential Democrats and to establish himself with the public as a national figure, Bobby's notebooks on the weak Stevenson campaign of 1956 were invaluable to him. The notebooks told of the need to set up a card file showing for each local Democrat information on his position, influence, family, likes and dislikes, religion, hobbies, and nick-name. There were also warnings about creating excellent press relations, appearing on TV only when he looked his best, keeping to schedules, mingling with crowds, and saying nothing that might antagonize any group of voters.

The final nine months of Jack's campaign for the Presidential nomination was signified by a meeting at Bobby's house in the Kennedy family compound at Hyannis Port on October 28, 1959. Bobby, who had quit his committee job a month earlier to become Jack's campaign manager, parceled out different parts of the country to a dozen aides as their area of work. In addition, he undertook to write an organizational manual so there would be no repetition of the mistakes of 1956 in the heat of 1960's political battles. As a campaign worker would later remark after reading it: "It's got everything from how to bring in the town big shot to how babies should be kissed."

Ordinarily, candidates and their campaign managers had to spend much time on raising money to finance their effort. But in the case of the Kennedy boys, there was no need for this because of their father's wealth. The elder Kennedy bought a plane for their use and paid for their large staff so that they could devote all their time to the goal they pursued.

Bobby's value to his brother was priceless. For one thing, Jack knew he was totally devoted to him and en-tirely unselfish in wanting him to succeed. He worked almost around the clock and drove his campaign staff almost as hard. For another thing, Bobby was willing to take all blame for speaking bluntly to local politicians when such shock treatment was needed. Some said he seemed to be threatening their political futures unless they supported his brother; others, that he used rude shortcuts to put his brother's campaign into focus. Once when he spoke to a group of Democrats, he cast aside all diplomatic pretense and said, "Gentlemen, I don't care if the state and county organizations survive after November, and I don't give a darn if you survive. I want to elect John F. Kennedy." Because of Bobby's selfless role, said Jack, "I didn't have to worry about anything except what I was going to say, which was enough of a challenge."

It was Bobby who convinced Jack of the importance of running in the Wisconsin and West Virginia primaries in the spring of 1960. When private public opinion polls showed Jack an easy winner over Senator Hubert Humphrey in Wisconsin, Bobby created a David versus Goliath myth by portraying his brother to newsmen as the underdog. This built up interest in the contest, and when Jack won, newspapers gave him front-page coverage as a candidate who had overcome great odds to emerge victorious. In West Virginia, Humphrey campaigned as though his opponent were Bobby, not Jack. He wailed that Bobby was spending hundreds of thousands of dollars to buy votes and that Bobby had spread the story that Jimmy Hoffa was behind Humphrey.

After his brother's one-sided victory over Humphrey in West Virginia, Bobby was certain Jack would win the Presidential nomination on the first ballot at the Democratic National Convention in Los Angeles in July, 1960. Nevertheless, from the start he equipped his large staff with walkie-talkies, called staff meetings at 8:30 A.M.

daily, and had his aides report in regularly until past midnight regarding the delegates to whom they had spoken. "We're not out here to go to Disneyland," he warned his workers. "And I want to hear only about the delegates we are guaranteed on the first ballot."

When Jack won the nomination on the first ballot, Bobby was opposed initially to his brother's decision to put Senator Lyndon Johnson on the ticket as the Vice Presidential nominee. In the politicking at the convention he had grown furious on learning that Johnson had referred to his father as a "Chamberlain umbrella man" (an appeaser), and his emotions did not cool upon hearing that Johnson's aides had spread the story that Jack was dying from Addison's disease. But eventually he became reconciled to his brother's choice because of the need for Southern votes in the election against Vice President Richard Nixon, the Republican nominee.

In the campaign that fall, aides were astonished that Bobby worked at top speed for eighteen to twenty hours a day. His long-distance phone bill for a single day came to $10,000. He determined every stop Jack would make in the campaign and how long he would be at each place, where he would appear on TV and what he should not say, and he kept the card-file data at his brother's immediate call.

As in the 1952 Senate campaign, Bobby was concerned about Democrats who were not registered and thus ineligible to vote. He hired 250 organizers in 1960 and assigned them the task of registering adult Americans in the northeastern part of the United States. A minimum estimate was that they helped more than 5,000,000 persons register.

Robert Francis Kennedy

On election night a pale, thin, and exhausted Robert Kennedy came to Hyannis Port to hear the election returns. He stayed up all night, keeping check on the reported votes as they came in on the close election. In the morning he was still awake, hollow-eyed but excited. "It's too good to be true," he exclaimed when his brother edged ahead of Nixon by 112,881 votes.

In the period between the election in November and his inauguration in January, Jack Kennedy decided that he wanted Bobby to hold a position of power in the federal government. The job he chose for him was that of Attorney General. The idea for the appointment had come originally from Joseph Kennedy, who believed Bobby should be rewarded for his work with a Cabinet position. Though Jack had offered the Justice Department post first to Representative Abraham Ribicoff, Jack selected Bobby when Ribicoff rejected it.

However, Bobby also turned it down. Besides the charge of nepotism that would be made, he argued, how could he become Attorney General when he had never been in private law practice or handled a court case? If he were to ignore nepotism, he went on, the job he really wanted was as Assistant Secretary of State for Latin American affairs.

Jack later recalled the final discussion they had on the appointment. The State Department post was out because Bobby would not be able to communicate directly with the White House but would have to go through existing channels. As a Cabinet member he could speak directly with the President. When Bobby continued to argue, Jack told him bluntly, "I have made up my mind and don't want to talk about it any more. You are going to be Attorney General." When Bobby at last agreed to take the job, Jack arranged a news conference to make the announcement. As they walked toward the door to meet the reporters, Jack turned to scold his brother: "Bobby! Please comb your hair!"

The expected press storm against the appointment failed to occur. Nevertheless, when Bobby moved into the spacious fifth-floor office in the Justice Department Building in downtown Washington, reporters paid close scrutiny to his activities. Some criticized his large black Labrador, Brumus, who frightened visitors to his office; others called him a hatchet man, who performed unpleasant duties for his brother, such as scolding government officials for misdeeds, rousing reporters in the middle of the night to demand that they be more accurate or that they tell him the sources for their stories. On one score there was no criticism: Bobby had hired the best legal brains in the country to serve in his department.

On the job, Bobby's chief activity lay in strengthening the legal rights of black Americans. When he first became a Cabinet member, Bobby admitted, "I wasn't lying awake nights thinking about the Negro in this country." A friend said at that time, "He is not for Negroes; he is not against them." But after viewing the pictures of police with electric prodding rods and trained dogs attacking civil rights marchers and sit-in demonstrators, his anger developed, and he became the nation's leading fighter against racial injustice. Even more important, he converted his brother Jack to his new point of view.

At the Justice Department, he added forty Negro

168

lawyers, named the first Negro U.S. Attorneys in history, and undertook a continuous effort to enforce the Supreme Court's decision of May, 1954, to end segregation in education. This meant that the public schools of Atlanta and Dallas had to integrate their pupils and that the University of Mississippi had to admit James Meredith, a Negro.

By June, 1963, Bobby went further and prepared a major civil rights bill that his brother sent to Congress. Among its features were those eliminating discrimination against Negroes in restaurants, hotels, and rest rooms; ending voting discrimination; and giving his department authority to speed school desegregation. Congress passed this bill a year later under a new President.

Bobby also spent much time studying the way justice was administered in the United States. The findings of a special committee he named revealed that the rich were treated more leniently in court than the poor. This led to legislation to establish free legal aid and lower bail charges for those at the bottom of the economic ladder.

As devoted as he was to expanding civil rights for Negroes and establishing justice in the courts for the poor, Bobby wanted to withhold equal legal treatment for those involved in organized crime. Some lawyers objected to what they called shortcuts in obtaining evidence. Old-line government employees in the Internal Revenue Service resented his order to drop their attention on finding small errors in tax returns of the average citizen and concentrate, instead, on catching big-time criminals through their false tax returns.

There were also editors who were appalled when he used his new position to continue his war against Jimmy

Hoffa. In 1959, between the time he had quit the McClel·
lan Committee and assumed command of his brother's
campaign, Bobby had written a book, *The Enemy
Within,* detailing his work as a committee investigator
and his troubles with Hoffa. This had proved a profitable
venture, for the movies had paid $120,000 for the screen
rights, all of which he had turned over to charities for
mentally retarded children.

Bobby's friends had assumed that with the publication
of this book he would forget about Hoffa. But as Attorney General he revived his interest in putting him in jail.
Not long after he moved into the Justice Department he
established a fifteen-man unit that became known as the
Get Hoffa Squad.

In October, 1961, the Justice Department won an indictment against Hoffa for alleged misuse of union funds.
Then, seven months later, Hoffa was indicted again,
charged this time with having accepted $1,000,000 from
a Detroit trucking firm and promising in return that there
would be no labor problems.

Trial on the second indictment came first, and Hoffa
was freed when the jury could not reach a united verdict.
But Bobby ordered his squad to keep Hoffa's troubles
going, and the Teamsters president was indicted a third
time, on this occasion for tampering with the jury in his
court trial. At his new court appearance, evidence was
produced that the Get Hoffa Squad had engaged in wiretapping and bribes to obtain their information. Nevertheless, Hoffa was found guilty of jury tampering in March,
1964, and sentenced to eight years in prison. Appeals
were to keep him out of jail until 1967.

Besides running the Justice Department, Bobby Kennedy was his brother's closest adviser in all fields of government. Sister Eunice said that the two "shared the Presidency." The British ambassador, Lord Harlech, who had known both brothers since the 1930's, commented that Bobby's "biggest value to JFK was that he was someone to whom the President could say exactly what he thought."

The two were on the phone talking to each other several times a day, and hardly a day passed without Bobby's rushing through the White House to his brother's Oval Office in the West Wing. Bobby was the recruiter who found the best personnel to fill important slots in the federal service. When a vital program lagged, President Kennedy called on Bobby to help provide it with steam. He was also the man to whom administrators flocked with problems and plans, certain that this was the best way to get the President's attention.

In foreign affairs as well, the President sought his advice on almost a daily basis. In the early months of the administration's first year, when Bobby learned of the extent of the Bay of Pigs disaster in Cuba, he told his wife Ethel, "I've got to be with him. I know he needs me."

In October, 1962, when the Cuban missile crisis neared its climax, the President asked Bobby to serve as his stand-in at meetings of the National Security Council when he could not be present. Members of the council said afterward that they were franker and more willing to argue the various alternatives when Bobby presided than when the President was in the room.

It was Bobby who convinced his brother that the best solution to the presence of Soviet missile bases in Cuba was not a surprise bombing of the sites followed by an invasion. He called this "a Pearl Harbor in reverse." The President's choice of the many proposals offered him by the council was the one Bobby favored. This was to establish a blockade of Cuba so that no ships carrying strategic materials could dock there until the Soviet Union agreed to withdraw her missiles. By coincidence, the first ship stopped in the Caribbean was halted by the USS *Joseph P. Kennedy, Jr.* When Soviet leader Nikita Khrushchev did not dispute Kennedy's decision, the crisis ended a few days later.

In the fall of 1963 Robert Kennedy spoke of quitting as Attorney General. He later gave his reason to a reporter: I'm tired of chasing people. I want to go on to something else."

Several of his friends were convinced that the "something else" he sought was the Vice Presidency in 1964. This would have made the first political ticket of brothers in American history. But whatever the probability of a Kennedy-Kennedy Democratic Party ticket under other circumstances, bullets fired at 1:30 P.M on a sunny Friday in Dallas ended the Kennedy administration with a ferocious suddenness.

From the time he first learned of his brother's assassination until his own death, the personal sense of loss to Robert Kennedy was enormous. During the first few days, which included the weekend of funeral ceremonies and the Arlington National Cemetery burial, he maintained a quiet dignity. But afterward great sadness settled on him like a dark night after a bright day. He could not work; he could not relax; he could not sleep. For a while he considered quitting his Cabinet post and leaving government service for good.

He was roused to a return to the realistic world in January, 1964, when he traveled to the Far East. Everywhere he stopped in Japan and Indonesia, crowds cheered him and wanted to hear about the fallen President. They gave him strength to survive the blow of Jack's death, and in discussing him, he found a theme for his own political future. In Tokyo he explained it this way: "My brother was not only President of one nation. He was President of young people around the world. If President Kennedy's life and death are to mean anything, we young people must work harder for a better life for all the people of the world."

On his return from the Orient, Robert Kennedy was once more ready to continue his public service. His ambition now was to become Vice President, and he gave as his reason: "I'd like to harness all the energy and effort and incentive and imagination that was attracted to government by President Kennedy. I don't want any of that to die. People are still looking for all that idealism. It permeated young people all over the globe. And I became a sort of symbol, not just an individual."

However, Kennedy's ambition ran head on into President Johnson's determination not to have a member of the Kennedy family on his ticket. Instead, he decided on Senator Hubert Humphrey, and his choice seemed a popular one among Democrats until Kennedy shyly walked onto the platform at the Democratic National Convention at Atlantic City on August 27, 1964. Delegates applauded and screamed, "We want Kennedy," for twenty minutes, while Kennedy stood before them and wept at his reception.

Having lost out on the Vice Presidency, Robert Kennedy took a vital step to remain in public service. "In order to do so, it was necessary to get myself elected this time," he said. "I had to run for office."

There was talk that he planned to run for governor of Massachusetts, but he chose instead to make the race for the U.S. Senate seat from New York. After he established his New York residence by renting a house at Glen Cove, a small town on Long Island, the New York State Democratic Convention overwhelmingly gave him the nomination he had sought.

Kennedy's opponent in that November's election was Senator Kenneth Keating, a highly regarded Republican who had served in Congress since 1947. The white-haired Keating's voting record made it apparent from the outset that he and Kennedy were in agreement on all important political issues. This unfortunately left Keating with little more than a campaign based on attacking Kennedy's personality and motives.

His chief theme was that Kennedy was a carpetbagger and had no business running for the Senate from New York because he was a registered voter in Massachusetts. A second theme of the sixty-four-year-old Keating was that his opponent was too young. "Maybe you should elect the oldest man in the state of New York," Kennedy replied. "And who grew up in Westchester County? I did. Keating didn't. Did he go to Bronxville schools as I did? No. Keating is the carpetbagger. He says keep New York's own. Imagine that. Boo boo Ken Keating. Boo

boo. Do you want a local boy in the U.S. Senate? That's me."

Still another Keating theme was that as Attorney General Kennedy had returned German property seized during World War II to their Nazi owners afterward. "I lost both my brother [Joe] and my brother-in-law [the Marquess of Hartington] to the Nazis," Kennedy answered. "I'm not making a deal with Nazis."

Kennedy proved an excellent campaigner on the streets, where crowds pressed toward him, eager to touch him. But on TV he came across with a frozen face, nervous gestures, and a high-pitched voice. This poor TV image was solved by having young people come to the studios and ask him questions. The change that came over him was immediately noticeable to viewers. "When he talks, he reminds me of his brother, and I feel like crying," said one.

The Kennedy clan, pouring into New York to help him with handshakes, tea parties, and speeches, was of great value to him. Ethel Kennedy, expecting her ninth child, walked through many sections of New York City to speak for her husband. She also made several telephone speeches in his behalf to assembled groups of women Democrats.

The cost of the Kennedy campaign ran into the millions of dollars, with $1,000,000 alone spent for TV in the month of October. But none of this spending was actually needed, for the opinion polls at the start of the campaign had shown Kennedy an easy victor over his opponent. Yet the polls had also shown that against any other candidate, Keating would have won reelection. As it was, Keating ran 860,500 votes ahead of Barry

Goldwater, the Republican Presidential candidate, in New York. Yet he lost to Kennedy by 720,000. Afterward Keating placed the blame for his own defeat on the fact that "we didn't have as much money as he had."

Robert Kennedy was thirty-nine when he took his seat in the U.S. Senate in January, 1965. Not far from his desk in the Senate chamber was that of his brother Teddy, elected to the upper house in 1962 at the age of thirty.

From the start, Kennedy found the pace of the Senate too slow for him. "They only take about one vote a week here," he complained, "and they never tell you in advance when it's going to be so you can schedule other things." Most of the work of the Senate was done in committees, with long lines of witnesses testifying on proposed legislation and committee members deliberating on legal language behind closed doors. Kennedy enjoyed the hearings, but he was impatient with the arguments over the language in legislation. One time, when two Senators were arguing over the wording of a sentence, he suggested that they "flip a coin."

What interested him most was to travel about the country with members of the Senate Labor and Public Welfare Committee, holding hearings and investigations on the problems assigned to that committee. His outrage against visible poverty in Mississippi and other places helped draw national attention to the substandard living to which millions were subjected in the midst of plenty.

Even though Robert Kennedy was junior in seniority to his brother in the Senate, reporters considered him the "Kennedy heir" and spokesman for those who had supported President Kennedy. If he and Teddy spoke on the same issue, chances were that his remarks, not those of the younger Kennedy, would be quoted. When he made a speech on the Senate floor, newspapers treated it with front-page importance, despite the fact that his short service did not give his statement much weight with his colleagues.

There was good reason for the newspaper attention, for editors were certain Robert Kennedy was pointing his efforts toward the Presidency of the United States. "I want to assure you that I have no Presidential ambitions, nor does my wife Ethel Bird," he joked with women reporters. But it was readily apparent to newsmen and fellow Senators that he hoped to become one day the second Kennedy in the White House.

For this reason, as well as the magic in the Kennedy name, he was treated as a national power by the press, instead of as a single Senator among a group of 100. Newspapers and magazines thirsted for additional coverage of Kennedy and his family to satisfy their readers. A favorite topic of political cartoonists was his long hair, which hung over his forehead like an embankment. Interviewers swarmed to Hickory Hill, the six-acre estate in McLean, Virginia, seven miles from the Capitol, to write about the Kennedys at home. The big white house on the grounds had been built in the 1820's and had been occupied by John Kennedy for a few years in the 1950's. In 1957 he sold it to Robert and moved into Georgetown, the social center of the capital.

At Hickory Hill, Robert Kennedy added a swimming pool, tennis courts, and riding stables, and by 1968 the house and grounds were crowded with the Kennedy parents, their ten children, a continual stream of visitors, and an assortment of animals that included ponies and a St. Bernard dog. Generally, when the Senate was in session, Kennedy rose at 7:30 A.M. and left for Washington by 8:30 after a horseback ride and breakfast. He had become so neat in his person that he changed shirts about six times during the day. He liked to be home for dinner and a half hour of family prayers with the youngsters before their early bedtime. Guest lists frequently included experts in a variety of fields, with Kennedy asking them leading questions and listening to their views.

While a Senator, Kennedy made several trips abroad, to the fanfare of more headlines, TV coverage, and large crowds wherever he stopped. Leaders of governments in South America, South and East Africa, and throughout Europe treated him as though he were the statesman from America. In talks to the people on his trips, he frequently shocked government heads by speaking his mind freely on the poor living and working conditions he saw. Often he engaged in direct dialogue with student leaders, mineworkers, and businessmen. In South Africa he openly attacked the government's policy of apartheid, or discrimination against the black community by the white minority. He told one white audience, "It was not the black man of Africa who invented or used poison gas and the atomic bomb, who sent six million men, women and children to the gas chambers in Europe."

When he had first come to the Senate, Kennedy did not consider himself a disrupter of the Democratic Party. "The business of parties is not just to win elections," he said. "It is to govern. And a party cannot govern if it is disunited."

But as time passed, he began opposing major policies of the Johnson administration, especially the war in Vietnam. It was Kennedy's view early in 1966 that the bombing of North Vietnam be halted and the parties involved brought together at the conference table. This position was finally adopted by the administration more than two years later. However, at the time Kennedy sponsored it, his words brought on a break between him and the White House.

Pressure began building on Kennedy from various Democratic groups to oppose President Johnson at the 1968 convention. Although he found fault with the administration on many issues, he solemnly announced his continued support for the President's renomination. Throughout 1966 and 1967 he repeated his support of Johnson, whom he considered unbeatable at the next Democratic National Convention.

However, his desire to wait until 1972 ended in March, 1968, when Senator Eugene McCarthy, a little-known underdog and a proponent of peace in Vietnam, shocked the administration by collecting a vote in the New Hampshire Democratic primary equal to that of Johnson. Before long, Kennedy announced his candidacy. Two weeks later he was surprised along with the rest of the country when Johnson withdrew as a candidate for reelection.

While his aides undertook the long and tedious task of gaining the support of Democratic bosses who controlled the selection of most delegates to the Democratic National Convention, Kennedy entered Presidential primaries in Indiana, Nebraska, Oregon, South Dakota, and California. He did so in order to convince the professional politicians he possessed wide popular support.

He realized that his first primary—in Indiana—was the most crucial, for a loss in the Hoosier State would eliminate him quickly from the race. The Kennedy clan came once more to help, and the former aides of President Kennedy turned to Senator Kennedy's cause. Crowds turned into mobs as his motorcade crawled down streets. They pressed forward to touch him and gain his attention. On one city street the happy crowd tore his clothes and chipped a front tooth, while bodyguards thought him fortunate not to have been harmed worse.

Reporters did not find him a commanding figure and personality. At a speaking stop, a newsman wrote, "He waited like a hunched schoolboy to be introduced. Even when he spoke, it was always tentatively, modestly and with deadpan jokes that turned on himself." Reporters described him as having a "Bugs Bunny grin." Yet they also reported that the young, the poor, and Negroes considered him their champion.

When Indiana Democrats voted in May, Kennedy ran ahead of McCarthy. But when McCarthy beat him in Oregon, political experts declared that Kennedy's fate would be determined in the California primary scheduled for June 4. Because of the size of that Pacific coast state, Kennedy had to conduct an exhausting campaign in order to meet even a small fraction of its eligible voters. Day after day his face grew more sunbaked, and every night he looked increasingly tired. His voice grew hoarse, and handshakes pained his tender palm. The crush of the crowds grew steadily worse, and aides worried about each stop. Finally, on June 3, after he put in his last fourteen-hour day, they breathed, relieved, that the California primary campaign had ended.

Robert Kennedy sat in his fifth-floor suite at the Los Angeles Ambassador Hotel as the returns came in during the evening of June 4. It was a happy time, for he was ahead of McCarthy, and he relaxed in the company of his wife, astronaut John Glenn, Olympic decathlon star Rafer Johnson, professional football player Roosevelt Grier, and other friends.

At last at midnight, with victory certain, he descended to the hotel ballroom to speak to his joyous supporters and campaign workers. There was humor when he pointed to big Rosey Grier and joked that "Rosey said he'd take care of anyone who didn't vote for me." There was also a closing note of seriousness when he said, "I think we can end the divisions within the United States. We are a great country, a selfless and compassionate country. So my thanks to all of you, and to Chicago and let's win!"

Robert Kennedy had planned to walk through the Embassy Ballroom for a news conference in another room. But the victory crowd was too solidly packed for him to make his way through the ballroom. Instead, helpful hotel staff members told him of another route through the pantry and kitchen area behind his speaker's platform, and he followed them in that direction.

A young Arab clutching a .22-caliber revolver had sneaked into the kitchen area earlier in the evening. Had Robert Kennedy gone through the ballroom, his wait would have been in vain. But now by chance the Senator suddenly appeared in the serving pantry, and the assassin's finger was on the trigger.

"How sad we are that we shall never see Bobby again, with his tousled hair, one or two children riding piggyback and another couple at his hand," said his sorrowful mother. "What joy he brought us; what an aching void he leaves, which we will never be able to fill."

# 5 Edward Moore Kennedy

SENATOR EDWARD MOORE KENNEDY—the last of the Kennedy brothers—stood before Bobby's coffin in St. Patrick's Cathedral in New York to speak for the family. His eyes brimmed with tears and his voice trembled as he eulogized his brother as "a good and decent man who saw wrong and tried to right it, saw suffering and tried to heal it, saw war and tried to stop it."

He quoted a well-known saying that Bobby liked to repeat as though the words had now been transferred to his own being: "Some men see things as they are and ask why. I dream things that never were and say why not?"

The sad farewell to Robert Kennedy was a reminder to those who knew the Kennedys well that Teddy, as the last Kennedy brother was called, had caught the baton from his fallen brother and would continue the

183

Kennedy race for political domination. "If anything happened to me tomorrow," John F. Kennedy had once prophesied, "my brother Bobby would run for a seat in the Senate. And if Bobby died, Teddy would take over for him."

Teddy had.

When their ninth and final child was born to Rose and Joseph Kennedy in 1932, the hopes of Joseph Kennedy for political glory for the Kennedy clan rested on the broad shoulders of Joe, Jr., almost seventeen years older than the newborn child. Yet the birth of Edward Moore Kennedy held special significance for the parents. He was born on February 22, 1932, the two hundredth anniversary of the birth of George Washington, and Joseph Kennedy was quick to point out this coincidence to friends and speak of it as a possible omen.

To Edward Moore, his birth meant special honors, for the infant was named after him. Eddie Moore, who had served as Honey Fitz's secretary, had gone on to spend decades as an employee and friend of Joseph Kennedy. He had served as Kennedy's chief helper in his Wall Street speculations and as a movie producer and undertook any assignment to enrich Kennedy or make his life more comfortable. A neat, trim white-haired man, he had once been described by *Time* magazine as: "Eddie Moore, Irish as a clay pipe, was the first member of the family Kennedy founded, nurse, comforter, friend, stooge, package-bearer, adviser, who played games with Joe and the children, bought neckties and bonds for Joe, opened doors, wrote letters, investigated investments, saw to it Joe wore his rubbers."

## Edward Moore Kennedy

It was Eddie Moore who had helped Kennedy ridicule a Vice Presidential candidate who specialized in championing the poor and attacking Wall Street operators. When the candidate came to Boston in 1924, Moore learned that he lacked transportation between speaking places and suggested to Kennedy that he lend the man his Rolls-Royce. "I denounced Wall Street from the back seat of a Rolls-Royce owned by a Wall Street operator," said Senator Burton K. Wheeler, the Vice Presidential candidate of the Progressive Party. "It occurred to me later on that Kennedy actually might have been trying to undermine me in this fashion."

It was also Eddie Moore who helped the Kennedys move from Brookline, Massachusetts, to Riverdale, New York, in 1926. Then, when these quarters proved inadequate, Moore was ordered back to New York from Hollywood by Kennedy to find a larger place. After Moore finished outlining what he sought, a real estate agent told him, "Kennedy can't use a residence. He wants a hotel." The place Moore finally selected was the $250,000 mansion in nearby Bronxville, where Teddy spent most of his early years.

"My first consciousness of how important Dad was to me began when I was allowed to crawl into bed with him in the morning and listen to him reading 'Donald Duck,' " said Teddy. "From our earliest days, I think all the Kennedy children were made to feel that our father's primary interest in life was his family. As the youngest, it appeared to me that the family was his only interest."

Another awesome family figure to Teddy was his brother Joe, who was a man in his eyes and the exacting

185

substitute father when his real father was away in Washington. Even before Joseph Kennedy found time to teach Teddy his philosophy that the only important thing in any activity was to come in first, brother Joe had already taught him this by using shock treatment. This had come during a sailboat race when twenty-two-year-old Joe had thrown five-year-old Teddy into the ocean because of his sailing errors that cost them first place.

Brother Jack, wrapped in his own activities, was also a man to little Teddy because of their fifteen-year age difference. However, Jack pointedly ignored the existence of Eddie, as he called Teddy in private throughout his life. On the other hand, brother Bobby, six years his senior, paid more attention to Teddy because of Joe's insistence, though sometimes with painful results. Ordered by Joe to teach Teddy to ride a bicycle, in typical Kennedy fashion Bobby took him to the top of a steep, tree-covered hill and started him down with a push. Teddy miraculously missed the trees, but, he said, "Inevitably, I crashed at the bottom."

In the spring of 1938, after President Roosevelt appointed Joseph Kennedy Ambassador to Great Britain, six-year-old Teddy crossed the Atlantic with his mother, Bobby, and their five sisters to live in the American Embassy in London. Happy, friendly Teddy, as freckled as his father, was the favorite of reporters. The *Daily Mail* on one occasion wrote about his puzzlement on hearing his father being called "your excellency," the term of address for ambassadors. "Is that your new name, Daddy?" Teddy was quoted as asking Joseph Kennedy.

Soon after his arrival in England, Teddy was enrolled in the Gibbs School, along with Bobby. But their father did not let their education interfere with the outside activities open to them as children of an ambassador. For instance, when President Roosevelt ordered Kennedy to attend the crowning of Pope Pius XII at the Vatican in 1939, he took his family along to Rome for the ceremony.

As Cardinal Pacelli, the Pope had come to the Kennedy home in New York for tea one day in 1937, when Teddy was four. The child had crawled onto his lap and asked him endless questions about the ring and cross he wore. Kennedy, Sr., had grown concerned about Teddy's questioning, but Pacelli had waved him off with a hand, enjoying Teddy's "interview."

When the new Pope now received the Kennedys and Eddie Moore, he focused his attention again on Teddy. "I wasn't frightened at all," Teddy reported afterward. "He [Pope Pius] patted my head and told me I was a smart little fellow. He gave me the first rosary beads from the table before he gave my sisters any." The Pope honored him still further the following morning when Teddy received his first communion from the head of the Roman Catholic Church.

Young as he was, Teddy was also put into association with the royal family because of his father's determination to make his job a family affair. "We all had tea with the Queen," Rose Kennedy said proudly. "The children got a great deal out of it."

Observers said that as the ninth and youngest Kennedy, Teddy lacked the feeling of self-importance and the competitive nature of his elders. When the other children were set upon by schoolmates, they fought ferociously. Teddy would not do so without parental permission. One afternoon he returned from the Gibbs School and asked to see his mother. Was it all right, he asked, if he punched a boy named Cecil? His mother asked why, and he explained, "Well, he's been hitting me every day and you tell me I can't get into fights because Dad is the ambassador."

Rose Kennedy said she would put his request on the dinner conversation agenda. When the subject came up, Ambassador Kennedy listened attentively to Teddy's story. "You just go ahead and fight back with Cecil," the ambassador said, "and don't be afraid that it will cause me trouble."

After the European war broke out at the beginning of September, 1939, Kennedy sent his wife and children home. A year later he resigned his post and came home, too. There he resumed urging his children to win races and show courage and instilling fierce family loyalty in them. With much of his attention centered on Joe, Jr., and lesser amounts on Jack and Bobby, little was left for eight-year-old Teddy, a chubby boy with a big jaw and a full head of thick brown hair.

Mrs. Kennedy once tried to explain why Teddy failed to get the same attention as the older children. "We tried to keep everything more or less equal," she said. "But you wonder if the mother and father aren't quite tired when the ninth one comes along. You have to make more of an effort to tell bedtime stories and be interested in swimming matches. There were seventeen years between my oldest and youngest child, and I had been reading bedtime stories for almost twenty years before Ted came. When you have older brothers and sisters, they're the ones who seem to be more important in a family and always get the best rooms and the first choice of boats and all those kinds of things. But Ted never seemed to resent it."

On occasion, his parents took unusual steps to show interest in this youngest Kennedy. For a time his mother pinned newspaper clippings on a bulletin board, and Teddy was supposed to read them and be tested on his reading during lunch. In another period his father ordered him to keep a daily diary and turn it over to him periodically for examination and criticism. Jack was then under fire from his father for his poor spelling, and Teddy was careful about his language. "You had to use words you could spell," he explained.

Yet while such activities gave Teddy occasional close ties with his parents in his preteen years, a continuing degree of separation was noted by dinners in the Kennedy household. Teddy and Jean had to eat dinner at the "small fry" table so they would not be present at the big table where they might hinder the loud political arguments between their father and older brothers.

Years later Jack told Teddy that he had an advantage being the baby among the nine children "because the discipline was breaking down when you came along." But rules were rules for all the children, including Teddy. When he rode his bicycle off the property and the news reached his parents, his father would rattle his newspaper and speak a few gruff words of warning; then his mother would lead him from the room and spank him with a wooden coat hanger. His older brothers also had rules for him that he found wise to follow. At Hyannis

Port he was supposed to rise long before them, run to the dock, and rig the sailboats they planned to use that day.

As children of a multimillionaire the Kennedy children enjoyed the good things in life. Besides the comforts of mansion living, seashore pleasures, and frequent weekends at the upstate New York farm, there were the enjoyable Saturdays when Joseph Kennedy would pile Teddy and the other younger children into the Rolls-Royce and all would be chauffeured from Bronxville to New York City for roast beef lunches at Longchamps Restaurant and movies at Radio City Music Hall.

Yet Teddy, like his older brothers at his age, grumbled at his weekly allowance, which his father at first set at ten cents and then raised to a quarter. Once, when he was eight, Teddy pleaded with his father for $3 so he could buy a used kayak. With a stern face, the elder Kennedy insisted that this was a large sum of money and that Teddy would no doubt grow bored with the kayak after a few paddles. Teddy's tearful expression finally moved his father to advance the $3, and the purchase was made.

The kayak became an object lesson to the boy. First, he lost interest in it after a few days, but it remained present to remind him daily that his father had been right. Second, the elder Kennedy cut his allowance by fifteen cents each week until he recovered his $3. In the summer following his kayak experience, Teddy sought to earn his own spending money instead of begging his father, and he gained personal satisfaction mowing lawns for neighbors and handling a paper route.

Like his brothers, Teddy was directed by his father

to non-Catholic schools. He attended several before being graduated in 1950 from Milton Academy, where brother Bob had gone. Teachers remembered Teddy not for the driving aggressiveness that had characterized Bobby, but for his friendliness. He also differed from Joe because he had to work hard in school for good grades. And he was unlike Jack, who had a quick temper and was not a warm person. What he shared with Joe and Bobby was his seemingly inexhaustible supply of energy. His sister Jean recalled that "even as a child Ted had a terrific animal energy. You never had to push Ted —you always had to hold him back."

When he finished prep school at Milton, Teddy accepted as a matter of course that he would begin Harvard as a freshman in the fall of 1950 and live in Winthrop House, as his three brothers had earlier. By that time having a son attending Harvard no longer thrilled Joseph Kennedy. The university had failed to award him an honorary degree. Furthermore, the Harvard alumni had failed to elect him to the Board of Overseers. "Bobby and Teddy didn't care much for Harvard," he later grumbled to reporters. "And I guess I have the old Boston prejudice against it."

Teddy had good reason for disliking Harvard because of a foolish misdeed in 1951, during his second semester. He had been having trouble with Spanish, and one day, just before an exam, he saw a friend who was proficient in the language and on the spur of the moment asked him to take the test for him. His friend was caught; both boys were expelled.

This turn of events shocked Joseph Kennedy. Jack Kennedy said of his father's reaction: "He held up standards for us, and he was very tough when we failed to meet those standards. The toughness was important. If it hadn't been for that, Teddy might be just a playboy today. But my father cracked down on him at a crucial time in his life and this brought out the discipline and seriousness in Teddy."

It was Joseph Kennedy's conclusion that Teddy should enlist in the Army, and Teddy did so in June, 1951. The Korean War was on, but Private Kennedy was sent to Europe for a two-year hitch in France and Germany. When he first landed in France, he was worried because he felt he had let his parents down. But he resolved to make them proud of him in the future.

He found the Army routine dull, of course. However, Europe was a fine place for weekend passes and leaves. During one leave, he climbed the 14,780-foot Matterhorn peak in the Alps. Another time he entered a bobsled meet in Switzerland, even though he had never taken a ride, and surprised his friends when he came in first. He also gained his first political experience in the Army when Jack ran for the Senate in 1952. "We have nine absentee votes in camp," he wrote his campaigning brother. "I like to think we got all of them."

By the time he was discharged from the Army in March, 1953, twenty-one-year-old Teddy had advanced to private first class. Once he was back home, he was determined to reenter Harvard and erase the blot on his record, and he was hardly out of uniform before he hurried to the campus to talk with the dean. Ordinarily, when a student was expelled from Harvard, he found himself permanently barred from readmission. However, Teddy pleaded with such earnestness that he won permission to resume his student status.

Now as a more mature student and older than most of his classmates, he worked hard on his studies and had no time for high jinks. He did best in public speaking and gained honors in government and history during his senior year.

Like his three brothers before him, he also had his eye on winning a letter in athletics. Standing six feet two inches tall and weighing 200 pounds, Teddy concentrated on football. At first he was satisfied to play on the Winthrop House team, which played other Harvard house teams and some from off campus.

One morning brother Bobby, who was then with the Senate Permanent Subcommittee on Investigations, was busily writing a report at his desk when the phone rang. He was seen to gulp, and after he hung up, he told the staff that a great emergency had arisen, requiring him to catch the first plane for Boston. Then he ran from the office.

Senators on the subcommittee believed a family crisis had arisen, and in a way it was true. It was Teddy who had called to report his desperate need for an eleventh player for the Winthrop House game against a Yale team that day. Bobby arrived on time, played the complete game at left end, and after Teddy's team won 7 to 0, he flew back to Washington.

Following the experience he gained on his house team, Teddy tried out for the varsity squad. Although the coach did not cut him off the Crimson squad as he did with half the other tryouts, Teddy recognized that his moves were slow and his knowledge of the fundamentals was mediocre. Again, like his older brothers, he talked several players into staying after practice and throwing passes to him. He also asked team captain Dick Clasby to give him tackling pointers, and he was so convincing that Clasby served as his personal tackling dummy.

All this hard work was to good purpose, for in his senior year Teddy won a regular end position on the varsity. In the big game against Yale in the fall of 1955, he thrilled the crowd by catching a touchdown pass. It was Harvard's only score, and Yale won 21 to 7.

Touch football games were the rage on the Kennedy lawn at Hyannis Port during and after Teddy's Harvard years. One weekend he brought two of Harvard's burliest linemen to the Kennedy compound, and they joined the game on the grass. Jack's wife, Jacqueline, was terrified when she clutched the football on one play and made a dash for the goal line with the Harvard two in mock pursuit. She finally fell and was carried off the field with a broken ankle.

When Teddy was graduated from college in 1956, he applied to Harvard Law School. Like Bobby eight years earlier, he was rejected. His first thought was to go to Stanford Law School in Palo Alto, California, but his father could not picture him so far from home, and he convinced him to apply to Bobby's school, the University of Virginia. A letter of acceptance arrived soon from Charlottesville.

To help Teddy spend the summer of 1956 in profitable fashion, the elder Kennedy asked friends at the International News Service to employ him as a reporter in North Africa. Teddy went abroad accompanied by Frederick Hollborn, his instructor at Harvard in political science, and they spent most of that summer in Algeria, then struggling in bloody conflict with France for independence. On their return, the two talked to Jack, urging him to speak out in the Senate against continuing American support of the French against the Algerian rebels. Not until July, 1957, did Jack do so, and his call for Algerian independence brought him widespread national and international attention for the first time.

It was inevitable that Teddy would be compared with Bobby by the professors at the University of Virginia Law School. Bobby was judged quicker and more argumentative; Teddy a harder worker and friendlier. Teddy's special friend was Varick Tunney, the son of Gene Tunney, the former world's heavyweight boxing champion. For courtroom practice, law students were given fictitious cases in what was known as moot court. Teddy and Varick won the school's competition at these contrived cases. Later some students said that Teddy had gained insight into legal action by his frequent visits to Washington to watch Bobby question James Hoffa. Teddy and Varick also took time from their studies at Virginia to attend the Academy of International Law at The Hague, in the Netherlands, in 1957.

Two important events occurred in Teddy's life during 1958. Jack was running for reelection that year to the Senate, and he asked Teddy to come to Massachusetts to help in his campaign. Teddy served as chief assistant to the campaign manager, who was Stephen Smith, husband of Jean Kennedy, and his job was to work on Jack's speaking schedule, talk to local Democrats, arrange parades and distribute thousands of copies of the *Reader's Digest* article on PT-109.

Jack's last speech of the 1958 campaign was scheduled at Dorchester the night before the election. When he showed up before the large and enthusiastic audience, he announced he was far too tired to utter one more speech. Instead, he asked for a show of hands from those who would rather hear him, Teddy, and Bobby sing a popular song called "Heart of My Heart." A critical witness judged their singing afterward: "They were awful!" Nevertheless, the three flat singing voices had no effect on the election's outcome, for Jack won the election. Much of his praise for this landslide victory was generously directed toward Teddy.

The second major event that year took place shortly after the election. This was Teddy's marriage to Joan Bennett, a pretty blonde who lived in his old hometown of Bronxville, New York, and was the daughter of an advertising man.

Joan was attending Manhattanville College of the Sacred Heart in New York when she met Teddy. The school frequently invited outside speakers, and the nuns tried to enforce a rule making it mandatory for the girls to attend the receptions for visiting speakers. Teddy was one of the invited speakers. On the day he came to the reception room, said Joan, "I had just skipped out, and one of my roommates came after me and called, 'You've just got to see who's there!'" Joan returned, met Teddy, and after a short courtship they were married by Francis Cardinal Spellman on November 29, 1958.

When Teddy got his law degree the following June, he wrote a letter applying for membership to the Massachusetts bar. In this application, he said, "My ambition lies in the public service of this state." Some in Massachusetts interpreted this to mean that he intended to run for the U.S. House of Representatives from one of the state's fourteen Congressional Districts.

But Teddy had something else in mind. After his graduation from law school, he made a tour of several Latin American countries, and on his return he plunged directly into brother Jack's campaign for the Presidential nomination at the Democratic National Convention in 1960. At meetings with his closest advisers and aides in the latter part of 1959, Jack parceled out sections of the country as areas of concentration for key helpers. Teddy was assigned twelve states, including all those touching the Rocky Mountains. There he was to work on influential Democrats and probable delegates to the convention to swing them behind his brother's candidacy.

In addition, Jack asked him to speak and shake hands in the states where the Senator planned to enter Presidential primaries. In Wisconsin, for example, where his brother and Senator Hubert Humphrey competed in the winter and spring of 1960, Teddy made the first ski jump of his life in the interest of creating local goodwill for his candidate. Fortunately, when he flew off the ski scaffold, he managed to land on his feet, and the cheers were loud. Senator Humphrey, after getting a résumé of what Teddy and other Kennedys were doing in Wisconsin, remarked, "I feel like an independent merchant competing against a chain store."

After his victory in Wisconsin, Jack called on Teddy to serve in the West Virginia primary as his substitute speaker for a few days. Jack had lost his voice, and the plan was for him to appear on the platform, nod and smile to the crowd, and Teddy would then make a speech. Once, after Teddy had delivered an emotional speech about the outstanding qualities a President had to possess, Jack stepped to the microphone and hoarsely told the crowd it had been obvious to him Teddy had been describing his own high qualities. But he wanted the audience to know, he continued, that Teddy was seven years younger than the minimum age of thirty-five required of Presidents by the Constitution.

To cover the vast territory of his assigned twelve Western states, Teddy learned to pilot a plane and barnstormed the area in a small propeller plane that could land on ranch roads. In every state he jokingly gave his word that he and Joan planned to move there and take up permanent residence. Just as he had gone off a Wisconsin ski jump to win support for Jack, he rode a bucking bronco at a Montana rodeo and managed to stay aboard for a credible five seconds. Only in Wyoming did he balk at taking extreme action. This occurred when he refused to hold a cigarette between his lips and let a sharpshooter knock it out.

Typical of the energy he poured out for his brother was his campaign in Wyoming, a state that he crossed six times in promoting Jack. Teno Roncalio, the Wyoming state Democratic chairman, was in need of a long rest after Ted's pursuit of his support. "He made me get up every morning and go horseback riding with him at six o'clock—and for an hour and a half!" he said.

Jack's praise for Teddy after his nomination was even more generous than that he had expressed after Teddy's work in his 1958 Senatorial campaign. To show how highly he regarded his younger brother, in his fall campaign against Richard Nixon for the Presidency, he again assigned the same twelve states to Teddy. Once more Teddy barnstormed, rushing in all directions to increase his brother's votes. But instead of joy on election night, Teddy was deflated when only one of those twelve states —New Mexico—gave its electoral votes to Jack. The other eleven voted for Nixon.

Teddy was among the large Kennedy gathering that came to Washington for Jack's inauguration. Newspapers stressed the youthful appearance of the new President, and some remarked that he did not appear to be in the tradition of American Presidents who were generally men of more advanced years. On his second day in office, President Kennedy was sitting in his oval office along with Teddy and Paul Fay, a friend from his PT boat days. Fay said: "I feel any minute somebody's going to come in and say, 'All right, you three guys, out of here!' "

Back in 1957, at a time when Teddy had not yet left Hyannis Port to begin his second year in law school, the *Saturday Evening Post* ran an article on Jack that contained the following: "Fervent admirers of the Kennedys confidently look forward to the day when Jack will be in the White House, Bobby will serve in the Cabinet as Attorney General and Teddy will be in the Senate from Massachusetts."

Strange as this may seem, by January 20, 1961, two-thirds of this prophecy had been fulfilled. As for Teddy, he was already aspiring for the Senate seat that Jack had vacated when he became President, and his father was his chief promoter, even though Teddy had never held a paying job since leaving school.

When the elder Kennedy first brought up the subject to Jack and Bobby, their reaction was entirely negative. Both sons quickly pointed out that the national outcry on nepotism would damage the administration. Joseph Kennedy later told a reporter he had chided his two sons: "You boys have what you want now, and everyone else helped you work to get it. Now it's Ted's turn. Whatever he wants, I'm going to see he gets it." To a family friend, Kennedy admitted that in his wrath he had told Jack, "I spent a lot of money for that Senate seat. It belongs in the family."

For the time being, President Kennedy reserved judgment on Teddy's ambition to become a Senator, though he made certain he did not close the door on his young brother. By law, the governor of Massachusetts was authorized to appoint someone to take the President's vacated seat in the U.S. Senate until the next Congressional election, which would come in 1962.

The governor of the Bay State was Foster Furcolo, a former member of the U.S. House of Representatives, who had fallen out with Jack during his Senate campaign in 1952. Their mutual animosity was so great that in 1954, when Furcolo ran for the Senate against Leverett Saltonstall, a Republican, Kennedy supported Saltonstall. In 1960, when Furcolo was governor and ran in the Democratic primary for the Senatorial nomination so he could oppose Saltonstall again, Kennedy urged his friends not to vote for Furcolo, and the governor failed to win the nomination.

After vacating his Senate seat, Jack Kennedy learned that Furcolo planned to appoint himself to the upper house. With the prestige and power of the Presidency behind him, he quickly objected to this and informed the governor that he would decide on his own replacement. Even if Jack had wanted to name Teddy at this point, he could not, for Teddy was only twenty-eight and the U.S. Constitution decreed that the minimum age for a Senator was thirty.

But he took the course best suited for aiding his brother. One morning, when Governor Furcolo answered the phone, Jack told him that the man he wanted named to the Senate was Ben Smith.

"Ben Smith?" Furcolo exclaimed. "Who is Ben Smith?"

"He's the mayor of Gloucester," Kennedy said. He failed to add that Benjamin A. Smith II had been one of his college roommates, or that Smith would serve as a seat warmer in the Senate until 1962, when Teddy would be thirty and eligible to run.

When Furcolo checked on Smith, he found he was not currently mayor of Gloucester but had held that post last in 1955. Nevertheless, he named Ben Smith to succeed Jack, and there the subject seemed to be closed.

With this successful maneuver completed, Teddy set to work to build what record he could for himself in the short time ahead. At his own expense, he tagged along with members of the Senate Foreign Relations Committee on a fact-finding tour of Africa. Before he started on this trip, he bought a large supply of brown stenographic notebooks, for his father had told him how important it was that he take notes on all he saw and heard. These notes could later form the basis of speeches he should make on the problems of Africa.

It was also necessary that he find employment and a

title. So on Teddy's return from the Dark Continent, his father's friend, Garrett H. Byrne, the district attorney of Suffolk County, Massachusetts, which includes Boston, hired the youngest Kennedy as an assistant D.A. The job paid $5,000 a year, but Teddy refused to accept the salary, and served instead as a dollar-a-year man. This was in the tradition of his older brothers, who gave their salaries for public employment to charity.

The next step was to dust off the script of Jack's race for the Senate in 1952 and follow it carefully. Brought back into the picture was Frank Morrissey, Jack's original political tutor and tireless Kennedy family aide, to do the same work for Teddy. Morrissey was now a Boston Municipal Court judge, but he found the time to arrange Teddy's first speaking engagements and meetings with Democrats in towns across the state.

After their regular day's work was completed, the two flew to an evening of handshakes and speechmaking, and Morrissey was proud of his pupil. "In the early years we had to shove Jack into the streets to meet people," he was quoted as saying. "Ted meets you and he just naturally seems to like you." Bobby, who watched his younger brother on one occasion, agreed that "Teddy is a better natural politician than any of us."

He showed his ease at politicking one time in mid-1961, when he strode through a Boston hotel lobby to shake hands. He was passing a private dining room and he poked his head inside to smile at guests at an Italian wedding reception then in progress. He was immediately recognized and surrounded. "You shouldn't be cheering me," he protested loudly. "You should be applauding this lovely young couple about to start a wonderful life together."

He then announced he had "a wedding present for this wonderful couple." His present turned out to be a flat-voiced rendition of Grampa Honey Fitz's favorite refrain, "Sweet Adeline."

Serious speechmaking proved to be more of a problem. His prepared speech on Africa turned out to be a miserable flop. On a visit to the White House he told Jack he was desperate and needed help.

"How long did you speak?" asked the President.

"Forty-five minutes. But I had a lot to say."

"Listen," Jack advised him, "if I can cut the State of the Union speech to twenty-five minutes, you can cut your talk on Africa."

Teddy did so with success. After this, he made a rule never to speak longer than twelve minutes.

There were other trips abroad during this period before he announced he was a candidate for the Senate. In the summer of 1961 he went to Latin America, and with the prestige of being a Kennedy, his talks and discussions with government officials, students, and labor leaders were widely reported by the American press. Not long afterward he made a third trip, this time visiting France, Ireland, Belgium, Greece, Poland, and Israel. Asked by reporters why he had made this trip, he said he wanted to study the effect of European tariffs on industry and jobs in Massachusetts.

Throughout 1961 the strategy was to have Teddy declare he was not a candidate for political office. This was considered necessary to give him time to develop a public image and save him from harsh attacks by other would-be candidates.

Joseph Kennedy was enjoying this smooth buildup of his youngest son as the year progressed, and after Thanksgiving he went to his Palm Beach, Florida, mansion, for the Christmas season. He was playing golf on December 19, when he suffered deep head pain on the sixteenth fairway. Taken to a hospital, he was found to have suffered a paralytic stroke.

Jack and Bobby flew from Washington, and Teddy came from Boston by military jet, bringing with him a specialist on strokes. During the elder Kennedy's crisis period, Teddy sat alone with him in his hospital room all night long, three nights in succession. When the crisis passed, Joseph Kennedy was alive, but he was left unable to talk, walk, or use his right arm. Nevertheless, his early thoughts were about Teddy's political ambition, and he managed to indicate that the names and addresses on the get well letters from Massachusetts should be put on file cards for Teddy's use.

Early in 1962 President Kennedy had to make up his mind about Teddy's future. Senator Ben Smith was telling friends he enjoyed Senate life and wanted to run to retain his seat that year. In addition, handsome thirty-nine-year-old Edward J. "Eddie" McCormack, the attorney general of Massachusetts and the favorite nephew of Speaker of the House John W. McCormack, was talking like a candidate for Jack's old seat.

At this point, President Kennedy had a private poll taken in Massachusetts to determine Teddy's fate. The results showed that Eddie McCormack would easily defeat Ben Smith for the Democratic nomination. However, the poll also showed McCormack losing to George Lodge, the son of former Senator Henry Cabot Lodge and the expected Republican candidate in the general election in November. As for Teddy, the poll figures had him beating McCormack in the primary and going on to defeat Lodge in November.

On reading this, President Kennedy determined that no matter how loud the charge of nepotism or Kennedy dynasty, Teddy would have his full support. Besides Morrissey's help, brother-in-law Stephen Smith, now an Assistant Secretary of State, was told to resign and become Teddy's campaign manager, the function he had performed for Jack in 1958. Smith was soon in Massachusetts, and his presence meant a vastly increased speaking campaign, large-scale spending on TV, radio, magazine, and newspaper publicity, and the establishment of a voluntary army throughout the state to work full-time for Teddy. President Kennedy also sent several of his White House aides to Massachusetts to help his brother, and to reporters he confided, "I'd rather be Ted than Ed." To all these activities by the Kennedy clan, James Reston of the New York *Times* had this to say: "Teddy's bid for the Senate, at thirty years of age, with the careful connivance of the President, is widely regarded as an affront and a presumption. In the end, it is likely to cost the President more votes in the Senate than Teddy will ever give him."

The Massachusetts State Democratic Convention was to meet in Springfield in June, 1962, to endorse a candidate for the Senate. This was not a final action, for there would be a state primary in September in which voters could accept the convention's choice or decide on another candidate. Nevertheless, the Kennedys considered the endorsement by the convention of prime importance because the winner there would begin the primary fight with more prestige than a loser would.

A total of 1,719 Democrats filled the seats of the delegates when the gavel sounded at the state convention, and there was some surprise when busy President Kennedy made an appearance on the platform. Stephen Smith was also present, though he was more often in the back rooms to promote Teddy. The rumor spread that even if Teddy lost, the President planned to put him in control of all federal jobs and spending in the state. Eddie McCormack's father, Edward J. McCormack, Sr., who was known as Knocko, helped fan the rumor flames by charging to reporters that "from the Kennedys, it's pressure, pressure, pressure—and postmaster, postmaster, postmaster promises."

Knocko expected Eddie to win the convention's endorsement despite the activities of the Kennedy forces. First of all, Eddie had by far the better background for the job. He had been first in his class at Boston University Law School, he had won election to the Boston Common Council, and twice he had been elected state attorney general, at which post he had made an excellent civil rights record. Second, Eddie had come to the convention with the combined backing of Harvard professors and dozens of local Democratic machines. One professor, Mark De Wolfe of Harvard Law School and an adviser to Jack Kennedy when he had been a Senator, had written in Eddie's behalf to 4,000 professors and teachers across the state. In his letter he had called Teddy's candidacy "both preposterous and insulting" and said that the choice before the convention was "between a bumptious newcomer and an experienced and gifted public servant."

But once the convention got down to work and the Kennedy steamroller shifted into high gear, Knocko's optimism turned into pessimism. Old friends began deserting his son and, on the first ballot Teddy easily won endorsement. However, Eddie McCormack was not through. Shocked though he was momentarily, he told reporters he expected to be vindicated when the people voted in the September primary.

For his strategy in his duel with McCormack, Teddy turned to Jack for help, and the President had three key suggestions for him. The first was the advice that he publicly confess having been expelled from Harvard as a freshman and not wait until McCormack's supporters spread the story throughout the state. Teddy did this, admitting openly that "what I did was wrong" and expressing his concern because of "the unhappiness I caused my family and friends at that time." As a result of Teddy's statement, the issue was put to rest and was never used by McCormack's backers.

The President's second piece of advice was that Teddy prepare himself carefully on national and international problems, so that when he was interviewed by hostile reporters, he would make no regrettable slips that would damage the Kennedy administration. For example, before he was to appear on the nationally televised *Meet the Press* program, Teddy flew to Washington for a dry-run rehearsal with President Kennedy. "He threw questions at me on every subject he thought they might ask,"

Teddy later explained as the reason for his flawless performance on the interview program.

The third piece of advice was the most important of all. On a visit to the White House, Teddy remarked that he had heard Eddie McCormack planned to attack him ferociously. Teddy boasted, "I intend to give him back twice as much as he gives out."

A frown settled on the President's face, said an onlooker, and he spoke bluntly: "You forget any personal attacks on Eddie McCormack. You're going to need all the supporters that McCormack has right after the primary. Stay on the issues and leave the personal attacks out."

Teddy put this advice to excellent use in campaign speeches and in the two TV debates he had with McCormack. The first TV "Teddy-Eddie Debate" was his crucial test, for McCormack was determined to destroy him as a candidate on this statewide show.

When they met for their debate in South Boston High School, McCormack lost no time pouncing on him. "What are your qualifications?" he hooted. "You graduated from law school three years ago. You never worked for a living. You have never run for or held an elective office. You are running on a slogan 'You can do more for Massachusetts.' This is the most insulting slogan I have seen because it means vote for this man because he has influence, he has connections, he has relatives."

While Teddy fought to control his growing anger, McCormack went on: "I listened to my opponent the other night and he said, 'I want to serve because I care.' You didn't care very much, Ted, when you could have voted between 1953 and 1960 on sixteen occasions and you voted only three times. Do you really care about civil rights? While I was fighting to eliminate the 'Black Belt' and the ghettos, you were attending a school that is almost totally segregated, at the University of Virginia."

As Teddy labored to maintain a calm expression, McCormack turned to him and called out, "And I ask you, if his name was Edward Moore—with your qualifications, Teddy—if it was Edward Moore, your candidacy would be a joke. Nobody's laughing, because his name is not Edward Moore. It's Edward Moore Kennedy."

Teddy ignored McCormack's personal attacks and spoke only about state and national issues. After the debate, newspapers assessed the results. McCormack had previously been accepted as the underdog in a race involving the Kennedy name and fortune. Now the average viewer looked on him as a bully and transferred his sympathy to Teddy. So McCormack's attack had boomeranged on him.

Besides the "Teddy-Eddie Debates" on TV, the two candidates programmed individual campaigns to take them into all fourteen of the state's counties. The difference in the style between the two campaigns was immediately obvious to reporters. McCormack had little money. He could afford few newspaper or radio ads; nor could he bear the expense of a paid staff or large local rallies. Posters that were nailed to poles and walls had to be hand-painted by volunteers. Knocko McCormack, his father, and John W. "Jocko" McCormack, his older brother, who supervised his volunteers, found them a dwindling army as the campaign progressed. By the end of the campaign, Eddie McCormack found few persons on hand to greet him at each town and tiny audiences to hear him shout his campaign slogan: "I back Jack, but Teddy isn't ready." He was forced to handle so much of his campaign's details that he lost 14 pounds in two months.

On the other hand, Teddy's campaign in the succession of Massachusetts towns was a merry scene of noisy brass bands, high-stepping drum majorettes, blinding searchlights, and laughing optimism. On some days Teddy made as many as forty short speeches at street corner rallies, sang "Sweet Adeline" on occasion, and performed Grampa Honey Fitz's stiff-legged Irish jig. Newspapers, radio stations, and TV channels were flooded with Kennedy ads, and to get the labor vote, the candidate walked through dozens of manufacturing plants to shake hands with workers on the assembly lines. "Teddy, me boy," one man called to him, "they say you ain't worked a day in your life. Let me tell you, you haven't missed a thing."

With the Kennedy rallies growing larger and the McCormack rallies smaller, long before primary day in September, 1962, the results were obvious. When the count was completed, Teddy emerged with 69 percent of the vote, collecting 559,251 to 247,366 for McCormack.

This still left the fall campaign against Republican nominee George Lodge and third party man H. Stuart Hughes. Newspapers labled this the Battle of the Dynasties, for Hughes was the grandson of Charles Evans Hughes, former Chief Justice of the Supreme Court. George Lodge, only four years older than Teddy, had the benefit of his family's wealth and political past and the prestige of having been an Assistant Secretary of Labor in the Eisenhower administration. Hughes was a representative of the teaching community, as a professor of history at Harvard.

The long two months of this campaign finally ended on November 6. Lodge's total vote was 863,400, and Hughes' column showed a mere 49,102. Teddy Kennedy was now a United States Senator, for his total was 1,143,021.

When Teddy came down the Senate aisle to be sworn in by Vice President Johnson on January 9, 1963, several Senators shook their heads at his presence in the upper chamber. In an editorial, the New York *Times* declared his newly won status to be "demeaning to the dignity of the Senate and the democratic process."

It was apparent to Teddy that he would have to work especially hard to gain the goodwill of his colleagues. First of all, their average age was twice his own—the oldest was eighty-five. Second, their backgrounds were impressive.

President Kennedy had sound advice for his brother. "Listen, watch, and keep your mouth shut," he said. He also told Teddy to avoid press interviews and news photographers and to concentrate instead on quietly learning his job.

Still further advice was that he go to the offices of the senior Senators, introduce himself in private, and praise that part of their Senate record with which he agreed. One old Senator kept him waiting in the reception room fifteen minutes after he was announced, but Teddy did not leave, nor did his face betray the rude treatment he had suffered. When he called on Senator Richard Russell of Georgia, who had come to the Senate in 1933 at the age of thirty-five, he tried to find common ground by pointing out that both had arrived as young men in the upper chamber. "Yes," Russell replied, "but by then I had already been governor of Georgia."

In his first year as a Senator, Teddy sat quietly at his desk in the back row during debate on legislation, and he put in hundreds of hours at hearings of the Senate Labor Committee, to which he had been assigned. When the Vice President had more important things to do than preside as an almost powerless figure in the Senate chamber, he sought freshman Senators to take over this chore for him, and Vice President Johnson frequently used Teddy as his substitute.

The young Senator was sitting in the presiding officer's raised chair and signing correspondence at 1:41 P.M. on November 22, 1963, when a Senate employee rushed to the dais. "The most terrible thing has happened. It's terrible, terrible," he called to Teddy and brought the debate to silence.

"What is it?" Teddy asked.

"Your brother . . . your brother the President. He's been shot!"

It was Bobby who told Teddy by telephone that Jack was dead. Bobby was in a state of near collapse, and he insisted that Teddy fly to Hyannis Port and break the terrible news to their parents.

Stunned though he also was by the catastrophe, Teddy undertook this sad assignment. When he reached the Kennedy compound, he learned that his mother already knew, though his father did not. The sight of his bedridden father with an ashen face prevented him from relating what had happened.

The elder Kennedy, sensing that something unusual had occurred, motioned to Teddy to turn on the TV set. But Teddy said it was broken, for he knew that every channel would be carrying the assassination story. Only in the morning, twelve hours later, was he able to muster the strength to tell his father. "There's been a bad accident," he blurted. "Jack's been hurt very badly." Then he added, his eyes filled with tears, "As a matter of fact, he died."

In the Senate session following his brother's death, the principal legislation was the Civil Rights Act of 1964. During debate on this measure, Teddy made his first major Senate speech on April 9, and he voted with the majority on June 19, when the Senate passed the bill at 8 P.M.

Teddy had promised to make an appearance at the Massachusetts Democratic Convention at West Springfield that evening. Shortly after the vote, he, Senator and Mrs. Birch Bayh of Indiana, and Teddy's aide Edward Moss took off in a small rented plane from Washington National Airport. Atmospheric conditions were poor in the vicinity of Barnes Airport outside Springfield late that night as the plane approached. Pilot Edwin Zimny came in for a landing, missed the airport, and crashed into an apple orchard four miles away.

First report to the outside world was that Edward Kennedy was dead. This was not true, though Zimny died in the crash and Moss the following day. Although suffering from torn back muscles, under the stress of the moment,

Bayh managed to pull his wife and Teddy from the wreckage.

At the nearby hospital in Northampton, doctors diagnosed Teddy as having two broken ribs on the left side, three fractured vertebrae in the lower back, and three broken bones that were supposed to give support to the spine. If this were not enough, he had also suffered a partially collapsed lung, and he lost so much blood that he required three transfusions.

Far from acting the role of an isolated bedridden patient, he made his small hospital room headquarters for several outside activities. "Jack took advantage of his hospital time, and so has Teddy," said Rose Kennedy, during her youngest son's convalescence. "Their father used to tell the children they had to force themselves to think, and both boys did a great deal of thinking in hospitals. Their father used to say even Moses went to the mountaintop to reflect. Their father used to do his thinking on long horseback rides, and the kids named his horse 'Mount Sinai.' "

One activity Teddy conducted from his hospital bed was his reelection fight in November, 1964, for a new six-year Senate term. His opponent was Howard Whitmore, a well-regarded Republican. But the assassination of Jack the year before, plus Teddy's accident, gave Teddy the full sympathy vote of Massachusetts citizens in addition to the normal Democratic total. As a result, he won in a landslide with 74 percent of the total, collecting 1,716,907 to 587,663 for Whitmore.

Besides directing his aides in his own campaign, Teddy phoned dozens of friends to volunteer their services in New York State, where Bobby was also running for the

Senate. Observers reported that "a Teddy army" descended on New York to work for his older brother. Still another activity in his hospital room was his editing of a book about his father. The title was *The Fruitful Bough,* and it contained the recollections of 113 persons who knew Joseph Kennedy. Teddy later had this tribute printed privately.

Teddy also made a continuing effort to keep himself informed on national and international matters. Two evenings a week he held seminars in his room with outstanding persons in a variety of fields, and late every evening he studied the documents they left him. Professors of economics came from Harvard to brief him on taxes, federal spending, and foreign trade. Others came from the Massachusetts Institute of Technology to discuss science education. In addition, Department of Defense experts explained the new weapons systems; Veterans Administration officials, veterans' problems; Justice Department lawyers, antitrust cases.

In December, 1964, he took his first steps in six months, and he was elated to discover that his spine had healed. Then, one cold January day, Senators of both parties stood and cheered as Teddy came through an entrance into the Senate chamber. A smile lighted his face and a PT-109 tie clasp was in place as he walked slowly to his desk, leaning on a silver-headed cane.

As his strength returned and he regained the 28 pounds he had lost, Teddy took on an increasingly larger part in Senate activities than he had during his first two years. In May, 1965, he served as floor manager for a proposal for the first time. In this instance, he had introduced an amendment to the Voting Rights Bill, one that outlawed poll taxes in state and local elections. The Johnson administration opposed his amendment for fear it would endanger passage of the entire bill. But Teddy would not drop his amendment, and he collected supporters and led the debate on the floor. He lost by a vote of 49 to 45, though he won praise from Republican Leader Everett Dirksen, an opponent, who called his effort "the best presentation by a freshman Senator I have ever seen."

It was natural that frequent comparisons were made between the two Kennedy brothers as Senators. As a rule, Teddy tried to operate in the quiet background so that Bobby could shine in the public limelight. This was because Bobby had set his sights on becoming President. The result was that even though Teddy might do far more work on a bill than Bobby, when success came, Teddy generously credited his brother.

The difference between the two also showed in their Senate speeches. For example, when Teddy spoke in favor of the Immigration Bill of 1965, he praised other Senators by name for having sponsored the bill originally. On the other hand, in his presentation, Bobby pointed out that the central core of the measure "was first incorporated in a bill drafted in the Department of Justice while I was Attorney General."

Teddy was a team player who learned to pace himself to the slow movement of the Senate. He was always friendly and generous, even when arguing with angry opponents. Bobby was too filled with impatience for such action. When a Senator continually interrupted a witness at a hearing, Bobby snapped at him before a

large audience, "Why don't you listen to his testimony and then criticize?"

"I have no objection to hearing his testimony," said the Senator. "But he loses me with—"

"With big words?" Bobby cut in, grinning.

With Bobby — and Jack before him — using their Senate positions as way stations to higher office, there was little question that Teddy was a far more effective Senator. Senate Majority Leader Mike Mansfield of Montana once observed, "Of all the Kennedys, Ted is the only one who was and is a real Senate man."

Even though he purposely kept his publicity down, by the fall of 1966 Teddy was regarded by members of his party and the public as a national figure. Dozens of Congressmen, who were up for reelection that year, asked him, as well as Bobby, to come to their states and campaign in their behalf. Generally, Teddy came with a few aides, while Bobby was followed by a planeload of reporters.

When Bobby entered Presidential primaries in the spring of 1968, Teddy gladly took time off from his Senate duties to make speeches for his brother and join him in campaign strategy. He was in San Francisco for the victory celebration as Bobby's substitute at Kennedy headquarters just after midnight on June 5, when word came that his brother had been shot. An Air Force jet flew him to Los Angeles, and he hurried to Good Samaritan Hospital, where the last hours of Bobby's life were swiftly fading.

It was Teddy's task to tell his parents of tragedy, and he called them at Hyannis Port. His mother

217

had already heard the news on TV. After their conversation and a long cry, Rose Kennedy put on sunglasses, walked to Jack's house in the compound, and bounced a tennis ball against the wall for ten minutes.

When his brother's body was brought to St. Patrick's Cathedral in New York City, Teddy remained almost the entire night alongside the casket. In the morning, exhausted and grief-stricken, he spoke at the services with a voice that was choked and eyes brimming with tears. Then on the train ride to Washington for the burial of Bobby alongside Jack at Arlington National Cemetery, Teddy found comfort on the back platform by waving to the hundreds of thousands of persons who lined the route to pay their respects.

The baby of the family was now the senior son— the last of the Kennedy boys.

That the Kennedy name still retained the sound of political magic was apparent early in August, 1968, when Vice President Hubert Humphrey begged Teddy to run on his Presidential ticket as the Vice Presidential nominee. The Kennedy name meant hope for a better life to millions, and translated into political terms, it meant sufficient votes to give the Democrats victory over the Republicans in the November election. However, Teddy's decision was a firm no to Humphrey.

At the Chicago Democratic National Convention near the close of that month, a sudden movement developed to nominate Teddy for President. Former Ohio Governor Mike DiSalle was already preparing his nominating speech when he received a phone call from Teddy at

Hyannis Port with the order not to do so. Teddy did not want any nomination out of sympathy for the Kennedys, friends said; he wanted to earn his future opportunities. Chicago's Mayor Richard Daley said that Teddy had been afraid to run because he mistakenly believed he did not have enough support. "Jack Kennedy knew how to count, and Bobby Kennedy knew how to count," said the mayor. "And Teddy had better learn quick."

During the week before the Ninety-first Congress began its session on January 3, 1969, a new Teddy Kennedy revealed himself. Instead of the quiet Senator who stayed in the Senate background, he now sought a leadership role in the upper chamber. The post he wanted was held by Senator Russell Long of Louisiana, a member of the Senate since 1949 and the chairman of the powerful Finance Committee, which wrote tax laws.

Long also held the position of majority whip, making him second to Majority Leader Mike Mansfield in directing the operations of the Senate. The primary function of the whip was to learn how each member of his party planned to vote on the important pieces of legislation and to help the majority leader bring all into line to achieve party unity.

Long believed he would be reelected whip without opposition at the Senate Democratic caucus, but a few days before it was to meet, Teddy announced he would contest him for the post. During one twenty-four-hour period, he spent most of that day phoning fifty-five of the fifty-seven Democratic Senators. The next day he called each again for support.

When the caucus began, Long looked confident, but when the vote was completed, his unhappy expression told the results. Teddy had defeated him, 31 to 26.

So Senator Edward Moore Kennedy moved from the obscure back row of the Senate chamber to the front row. The symbolism of this shift was not lost on his party or the nation. The last of the Kennedys had begun his move toward the Presidency of the United States.

But then, as had happened so often to the Kennedys, tragedy again struck Teddy. On the night of July 18, 1969, the car he was driving plunged off a bridge on Chappaquiddick Island, not far from the Kennedy home on Cape Cod. The only passenger, Mary Jo Kopechne, who had served as an aide to Bobby before his death, was drowned. Somehow Teddy struggled free of the submerged auto. Though he made repeated efforts to save Miss Kopechne, he could not reach her in the swift current.

After a week of silent grief, Teddy Kennedy went before a nationwide television audience and described what had happened. While taking full blame, he asked the voters of Massachusetts in effect whether the accident indicated to them that he was not sufficiently responsible to continue in the Senate. By letters and telegrams they endorsed him overwhelmingly.

So he returned to his duties in the Senate. But he made it clear he would not be a nominee for the Presidency in 1972. Yet what of 1976? Had the Kennedy path toward the White House ended forever? Only the passage of years would tell.

# Index

## The Author

Alfred Steinberg, the author of numerous books and articles published in national magazines, has contributed a dozen popular biographies to the Putnam's *Lives to Remember* series. He lives in Silver Spring, Maryland, close to the historical resources and current political scene in the nation's capital.

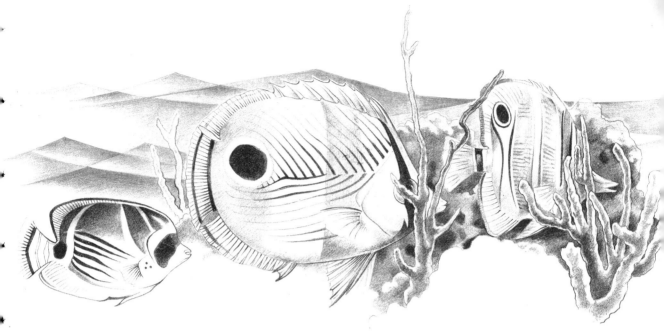

# FISHES
# THAT
# HIDE

CUMBERLAND COUNTY LIBRARY,
BRIDGETON, N. J.

### ALAN MARK FLETCHER

#### ILLUSTRATED BY
### JEAN DAY ZALLINGER

⟐ ADDISON-WESLEY

*Addisonian Press titles*
*by Alan Mark Fletcher*

**Fishes Dangerous to Man**
**Fishes That Travel**
**Fishes That Hide**

 *An Addisonian Press Book*

Text Copyright © 1973 by Alan Mark Fletcher
Illustrations Copyright © 1973 by Jean Day Zallinger
All Rights Reserved
Addison-Wesley Publishing Company, Inc.
Reading, Massachusetts 01867
Printed in the United States of America
First Printing

HA/BP        9/73        02030

Library of Congress Cataloging in Publication Data

Fletcher, Alan Mark.
    Fishes that hide.
    SUMMARY: Describes the different ways fishes camouflage
themselves to escape from enemies and to catch food.
    "An Addisonian Press book."
    1. Fishes—Juvenile literature.   2. Camouflage
(Biology)—Juvenile literature.   [1. Fishes.
2. Camouflage (Biology)]   I. Zallinger, Jean Day,
illus.   II. Title.
QL617.2.F56        597'.05        72–4767
ISBN 0–201–02030–X

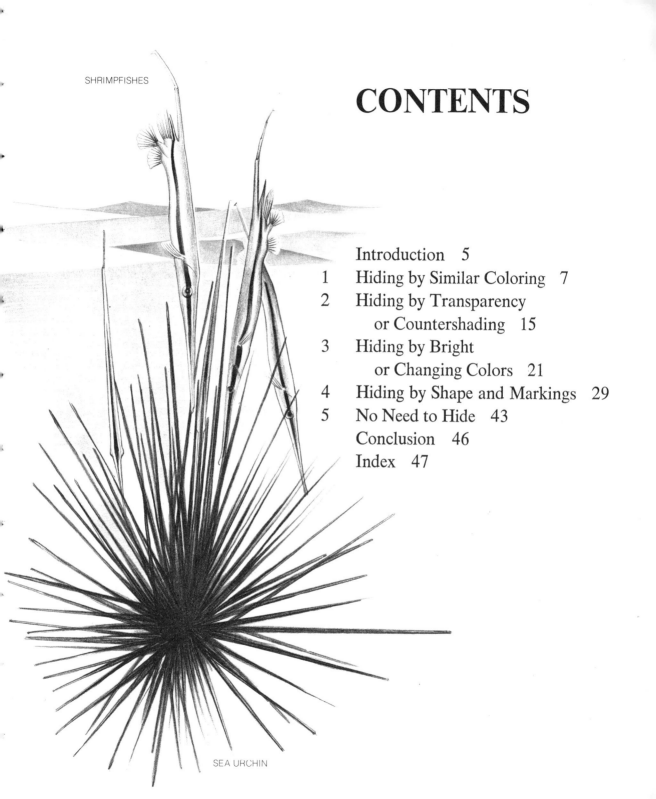

SHRIMPFISHES

# CONTENTS

SEA URCHIN

BUTTERFLY FISH

BLUE-GREEN DAMSELFISHES

# INTRODUCTION

## *Why Do Fishes Hide?*

Nearly all fishes hide. In fact, next to the insects, fishes are the best hiders in the animal kingdom. Some fishes hide to escape from their enemies, and some to catch food. Some hide for both purposes. There is another word for the way to hide: *camouflage*. Fishes that are hard to see are said to be camouflaged.

THREE-STRIPE DAMSELFISHES

BI-COLOR DAMSELFISHES

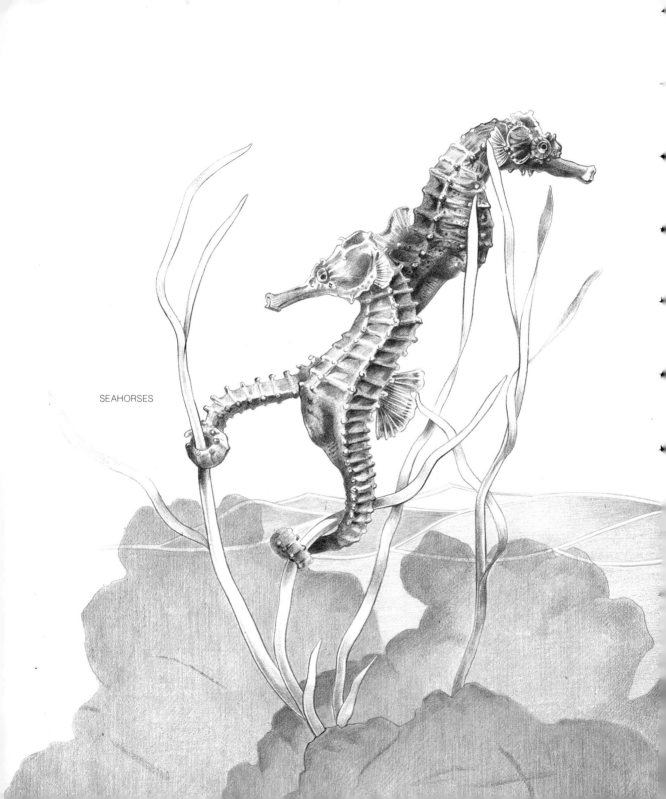

SEAHORSES

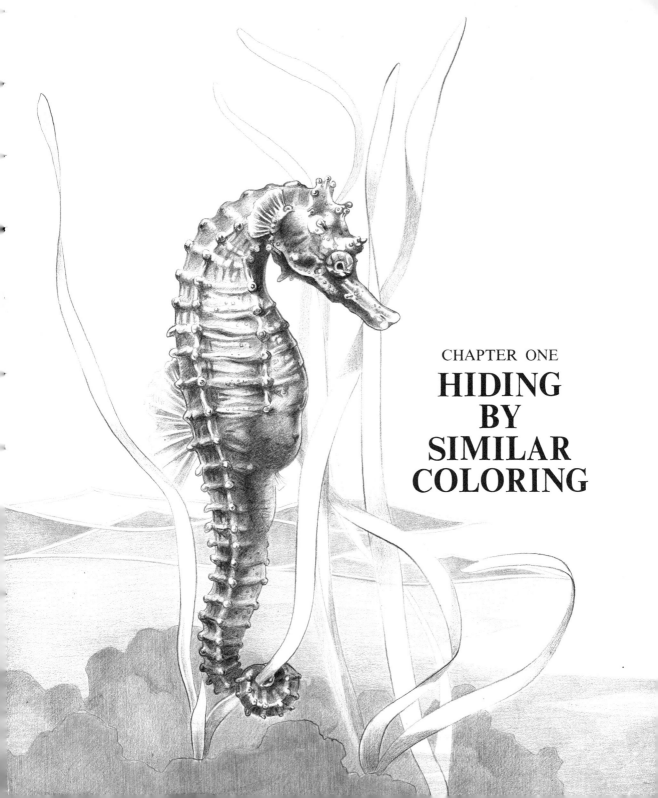

CHAPTER ONE
# HIDING BY SIMILAR COLORING

## On the Bottom

Many kinds of fishes are able to hide because their colors or shapes look like their surroundings. Let us think about some examples of this type of camouflage.

The oyster toadfish is found along the east coast of the United States. It has to be one of the ugliest fishes in the world. The large flat head is topped with two beady eyes and a huge mouth that goes all the way around the head. The leathery, warty brown skin and large head really make it look like a toad. But its ugly appearance is very helpful. The toadfish lives on the ocean floor and it is quite hard to see this fish next to the brown, muddy bottom.

Often the toadfish partly covers itself with mud and stones. This kind of camouflage is not for hiding from enemies but for finding food. The toadfish hides while waiting for the small fishes it likes to eat. When a small fish swims in front of its head, the toadfish opens its wide mouth and catches its food before it can escape.

8

OYSTER
TOADFISH

## In Seaweed

There are many small fishes that live in the oceans. Some of them never come close to land. One such fish is the three-inch-long sargassum fish. It is found throughout the warmer parts of the Atlantic Ocean. This fish lives among masses of floating seaweed which are colored in very pretty shades of brown, gold, and white.

The body and fins of the sargassum fish are almost the same color as the seaweed. When this little fish remains still among the weeds, it is very difficult to see.

The sargassum fish, like the toadfish, hides so that it can catch food. This fish can eat others nearly as large as itself. All around its head are yellow growths that look as though they would be good to eat. In fact, they look so tasty that other fishes swim up and try to eat them. Any fish that nibbles on the sargassum fish's head is quickly eaten.

SARGASSUM FISH

### *Fins and Tails*

The camouflage of seahorses helps them when they hide from their enemies. It also helps when they try to catch food. Most seahorses are the same colors as the ocean plants they live among. They curl their tails around a plant and can remain perfectly still for long periods of time. Even when they swim, they are very difficult to see, because they swim very slowly, and only their transparent (clear) fins move.

Some seahorses, like the sargassum fish, have growths around their bodies. These growths also help this fish to hide because they look just like the seaweed and other plants which are in the water. Other fishes swimming nearby have a hard time telling the seahorses from the plants.

*11*

## Swimming Upside-Down

The shrimpfish of the Indian Ocean is a thin, narrow fish with a dark black line running the length of its head and body. By itself the black line would not be very much help to the shrimpfish. But the shrimpfish swims with its head pointed toward the bottom of the sea. In other words, it is swimming nearly upside-down, or tail up. At first glance, a shrimpfish looks like a black stick on the bottom of the ocean. Sometimes, these fish travel in schools. When all of them swim together with their heads pointing downward, a school of shrimpfish looks like a large group of sticks.

SHRIMPFISHES

12

SEA URCHIN

Shrimpfish often stay among the long sharp spines of the sea urchin. This sea animal helps to protect the shrimpfish. The fish's black stripe looks just like one of the urchin's spines.

Other fishes are not likely to attack a shrimpfish hiding with a sea urchin. If they tried to catch one, they might receive a sharp jab from the spines of the urchin. A fish that has been stuck by a sea urchin probably won't attack a shrimpfish again.

GLASSFISHES

# CHAPTER TWO

# HIDING
# BY
# TRANSPARENCY
# OR
# COUNTERSHADING

We have already seen that some fishes, like the seahorse, can hide partly because their fins are transparent. There are several kinds of fishes that can hide because they are transparent nearly all over. Two of these are often seen in home aquariums.

The glass catfish of southern Asia looks like a thin knife blade. This fish is so transparent that you must look closely to see what its true shape is. Inside the very front of the glass catfish is a silvery sac. This sac holds all of the fish's organs. From the sac you can see the backbone which extends to the tail. You can look right through the rest of the fish to whatever is beyond it. When the glass catfish is swimming among plants, it is very difficult to see.

Another fish that can hide easily because it is transparent is the glassfish of India. Like the glass catfish, the sac containing the organs and the backbone are easily seen. Fully grown, it is about the size of a quarter. It has very large shiny eyes. Even though its bright eyes call attention to it, the glassfish hides well enough to escape from its enemies most of the time.

16

GLASS CATFISH

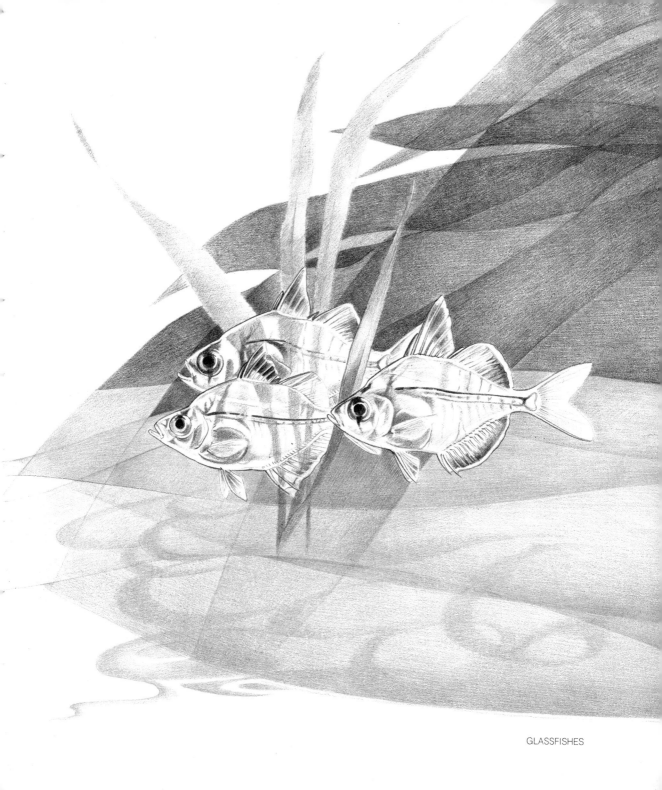

GLASSFISHES

18

TUNA FISHES

## Countershading

One kind of camouflage is found in nearly all fishes. Look closely at almost any fish. It is darker on its topside and lighter on its bottomside. This kind of camouflage is called *countershading,* or opposite coloring. It helps fishes to blend into the waters where they live. Here's how it works.

Sunlight, which shines on the water from above, blends in with the light color on the bottom of the fish's body. An enemy swimming below the fish sees only the light from the water's surface. The opposite is also true. A bird flying above sees the dark color of the water below. This darkness blends in with the dark top part of the fish's body. So you see, countershading helps the fish to hide from its enemies both below and above the surface of the water.

The upside down catfish from western Africa is darker on the bottom and not dark on the top like most other fishes. This is puzzling until you see these little catfish in an aquarium. They usually swim upside down! This is counter-shading in reverse.

19

UPSIDE DOWN CATFISH

ZEBRA FISHES

CHAPTER THREE
# HIDING
# BY
# BRIGHT
# OR
# CHANGING
# COLORS

Many kinds of fishes have bright or bold markings. At first glance it looks as though these colors make them stand out. But in fact, these colors and markings really make it more difficult for their enemies to see them. Such fishes are said to have *disruptive coloration.* This is what the bold colors do; they disrupt or hide the shape of the fish. Their brightness becomes a kind of disguise.

The cardinal tetra from northern Brazil is a very brightly colored fish that is often kept in aquariums. It has a shiny blue stripe and a bright red stripe on each side. In an aquarium the cardinal tetra really stands out. Such coloring might appear to make the cardinal tetra an easy target for any hungry fish that swims near. But in the streams where it lives, this is not true. When an enemy fish swims past a group of cardinal tetras, all it sees is a lot of bright red and blue stripes. It is very hard to tell one fish from the other. And it's possible that an enemy will swim right on without realizing that it has even been looking at other fish.

22

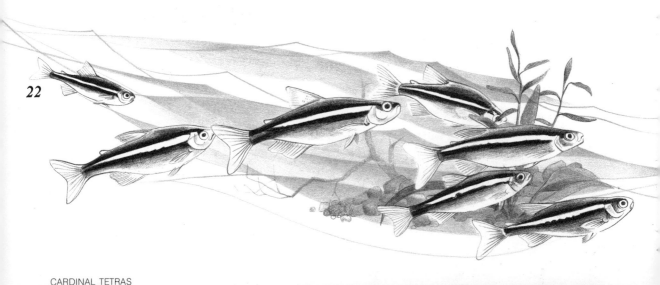

CARDINAL TETRAS

One popular aquarium fish that a lot of people like is the zebra fish from India. It has many dark blue and white stripes running the whole length of its body. There are even stripes on the tail fin. In an aquarium it is quite easy to spot this fish. But like the cardinal tetra, the stripes sometimes camouflage the zebra fish and protect it from being eaten by its enemies. When another fish comes close to a school of zebra fishes, all it sees is a lot of stripes. Many times it will just swim on by.

The little two-inch black-and-white damselfish from the South Pacific Ocean has very bold black and white stripes that run from the top of its body to the bottom. One black stripe runs through the eye. Two others run across the sides and onto the top and bottom fins. The tail fin is transparent and is nearly invisible. Because of the bold stripes, it is very difficult to tell one damselfish from another.

23

## Schooling

There is another kind of camouflage which is almost the same as disruptive coloration. It is called schooling. Many fishes, including the three you just read about, damselfishes, zebra fishes, and cardinal tetras, swim in large schools of their own kind. Sometimes there are hundreds of fishes in a school. It would seem that a large school of fish would be easy prey for a hungry enemy fish. But the opposite is true. To prove our point, let us imagine a large school of damsel-fishes. When they are seen together there is just a lot of black and white stripes. It is very hard to tell one fish from another. If a strange fish swims into a school of damselfishes, they quickly move away in all directions. The uninvited fish is confused by the fast movement of so many stripes. If it is lucky it might catch one damselfish. But all of the others will probably get away. Then as soon as the enemy fish is gone, the damselfishes come together to form their school again.

When both disruptive coloration and schooling are used together, they become a very good kind of camouflage. Without this protection, fishes like cardinal tetras, zebra fishes and damselfishes would soon be eaten by the others. In a short time none would be left.

CARDINAL TETRAS

GROUPER

PORKFISHES

## *Changing Colors*

Because it is sometimes sold as a pet, most people know about the American chameleon. It is a small lizard from the southeastern United States. This animal can turn from green to brown or gray. Some fishes also go through many color changes. One fish from India, the badis, is called the chameleon of the aquarium. The badis changes its colors so often that it is very hard to say what the fish's real color is. Within a short time it may be black, red, blue or white, or a few of these colors in patterns. It may suddenly develop stripes or bars in several shades. Whatever colors or patterns a badis appears to be, you may be sure that it will soon change to something else. These color changes are a great help to the badis when it needs to hide from enemy fishes.

The flounders and other flatfishes are nearly as good at changing colors but in a slightly different way. Flounders are found in many bodies of water all over the world but mostly in the ocean. All of the flatfishes swim on their sides, flat against the sea bottom. The side of the fish that is closest to the bottom is nearly white. The side farthest away from the ocean floor is usually brown. However, the flounder can change its colors to match the bottom almost perfectly. If it is on a tan sandy bottom, the flounder turns tan. If it is on a bottom covered with stones of many shades, the flounder will look like the pattern of the stones.

Scientists have found that if a flounder is placed on a black surface with white spots, it will begin to darken and develop white spots of the same size. The scientists have proven that a flounder depends on its sight for the colors or markings it will become. If a flounder's eyes are covered, it will not blend into its background.

FLOUNDER

ANGEL FISHES

CHAPTER FOUR
# HIDING
# BY
# SHAPE
# AND
# MARKINGS

One aquarium fish which many people have is the angel fish. This fish is very easy to see in a tank of water. But angel fish are from the streams and lakes of South America. There they can hide very easily among the plants which grow out of the water.

Angel fish have two advantages for living in weedy places: markings and shape. Among the weeds, the black lines that run across their bodies and fins are good camouflage. Sometimes these black lines can be mistaken for the weeds. And their high, thin shape allows them to swim between the plants, where larger fishes cannot find them.

The jungles of South America have many beautiful rivers and streams. Forests of trees taller than most of you have ever seen line the rivers. Because of the great trees, there are always dead leaves lying about in the water. But if you were to collect the dead leaves in a net, you would find that every once in a while one of the leaves might turn out to be a leaf fish.

The color of a leaf fish may be brown or gray, but the shape is always like a leaf. From the eye run dark lines that look like the veins of a leaf. On the fish's chin is a short flap of skin that looks like a stem. When the leaf fish swims, only the side fins and the clear tops of the back and bottom fins move. With such good camouflage to hide it, other fishes are always making the mistake of swimming too close to it. Often the unaware fish is quickly caught and swallowed.

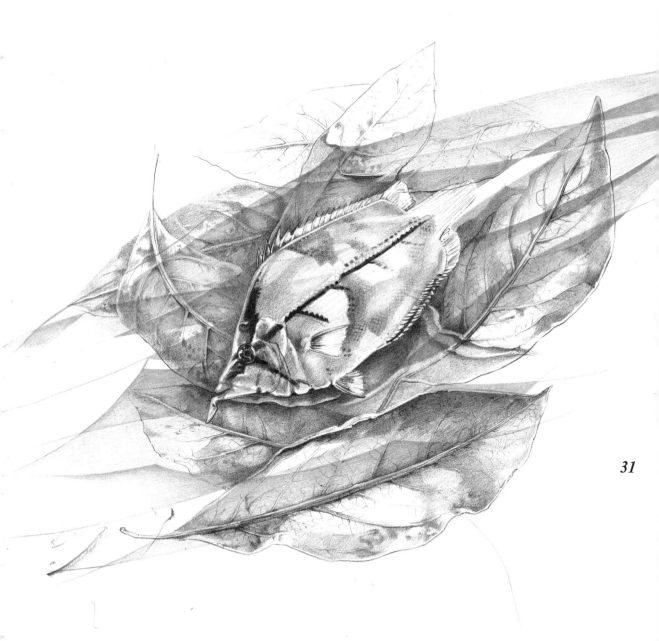

LEAF FISH

## Lines Through the Eyes

The eyes are just about the easiest part of a fish to see. Look at a guppy or a goldfish. You will probably see that the eyes stand out more than any other part of its body. The eyes of many fishes are camouflaged by a dark line running through them. Some are well-known aquarium fishes.

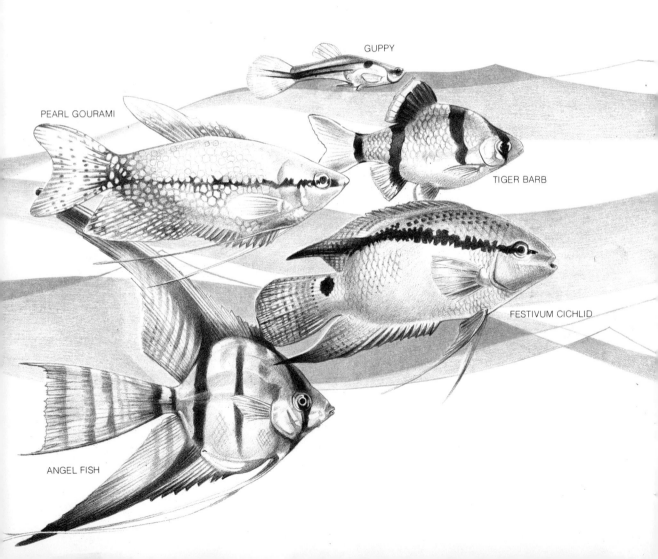

GUPPY

PEARL GOURAMI

TIGER BARB

FESTIVUM CICHLID

ANGEL FISH

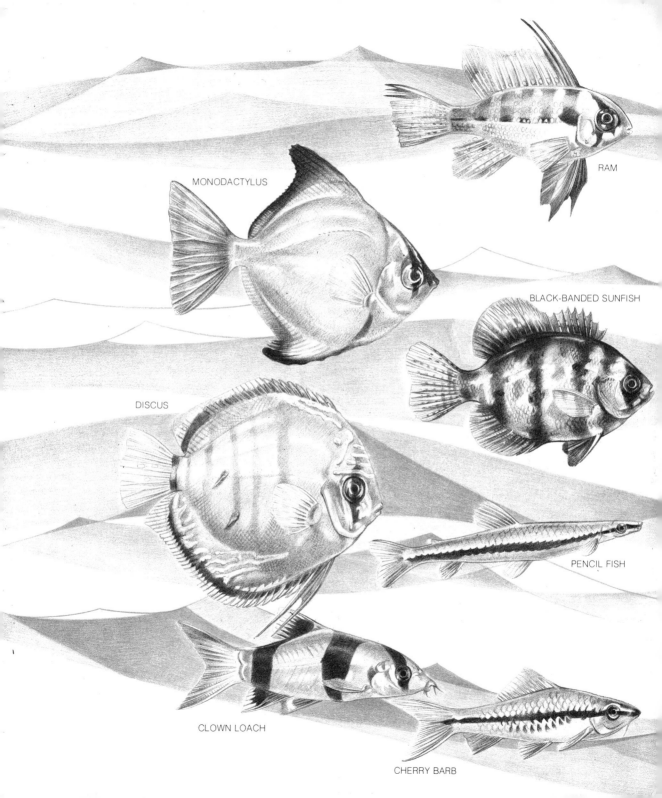

RAM

MONODACTYLUS

BLACK-BANDED SUNFISH

DISCUS

PENCIL FISH

CLOWN LOACH

CHERRY BARB

## Eyespots

The eyes of some fishes are hidden by false eyespots. These can be found near the fish's tail. You may wonder how an easily seen eyespot can help a fish to hide. They are useful for two reasons. First, the eyespot is larger than the real eye. An enemy that suddenly comes upon one is likely to think that the fish is larger than it really is. If the enemy believes the fish is too large to be eaten, it will pass on without attacking. This is an example of camouflage that could trick a fish's enemies.

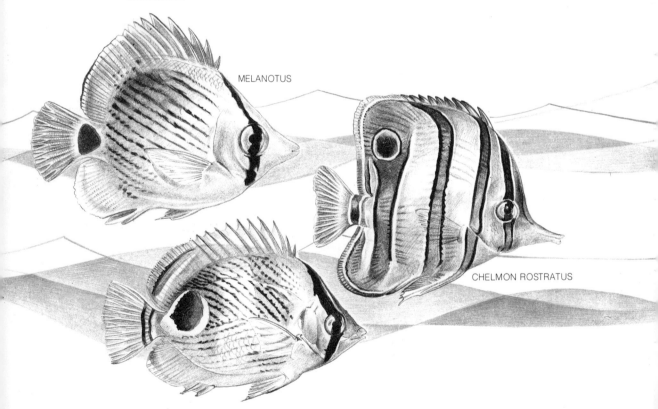

MELANOTUS

CHELMON ROSTRATUS

CHAETODON CAPISTRATUS

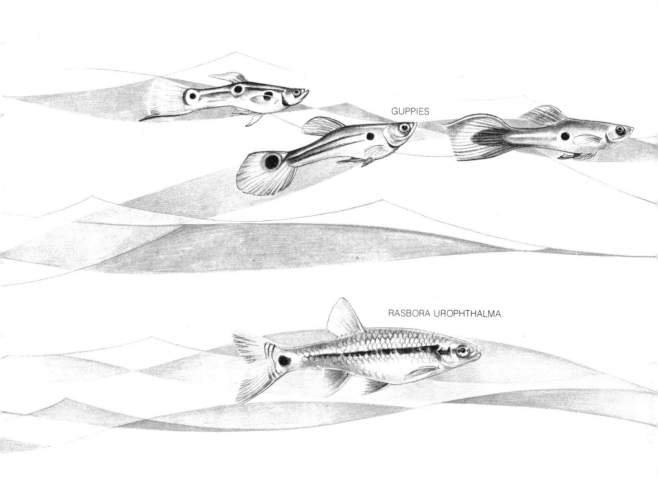

GUPPIES

RASBORA UROPHTHALMA

The second advantage is because eyespots are usually found near the tail. In most cases, when a fish attacks another one, it usually aims for the victim's head. When this happens the fish being attacked often backs up before swimming away. This movement slows his escape down. Now suppose an eyespot makes the enemy think that the tail is the head. As the fish is attacked near its tail, it can swim forward very quickly. It may even escape from the hungry enemy.

SADDLEBACKS

LONG-NOSE BUTTERFLY FISH

BLUE-STRIPED BUTTERFLY FISH

The butterfly fishes found around coral reefs all over the world are among the most colorful fishes to be found anywhere. Many of them have beautiful eyespots. Some of them also have dark lines that hide their real eyes. The largest eyespot found on any butterfly fish is on the saddleback butterfly. The jet black spot on this fish covers most of the back fin and part of the back. This makes a saddleback butterfly appear to be much larger than it really is.

Several of the fishes seen in home aquariums also have eyespots. Male guppies have bold black spots on their bodies or fins. Such spots could surprise attacking fishes just long enough to give guppies a chance to escape.

*37*

A pretty fish from Southeast Asia, called a Rasbora, has a white back fin with a large black spot on it. A black spot on the back fin may be better camouflage than a spot near the tail. An enemy that mistakes the Rasbora's eyespot for a real eye will bite over the top of this little fish. While the enemy is turning around to bite again, the Rasbora has more of a chance to escape.

One of the most frightening eyespot patterns is found on the twin-spot wrasse from the South Pacific Ocean. The wrasse has *two* huge black spots on each side of its back fin. Around each black spot is a white line and a black line. On the bottom of each spot is a large red mark. When a fish comes upon a twin-spot wrasse, it is probably as surprised as you would be by a Halloween mask!

Experiments by scientists have shown that eyespots are very good camouflage. They do not fool an enemy every time. But they usually mislead or surprise one long enough to give the victim a chance to get away.

*38*

RASBORA DORSIOCELLATUS

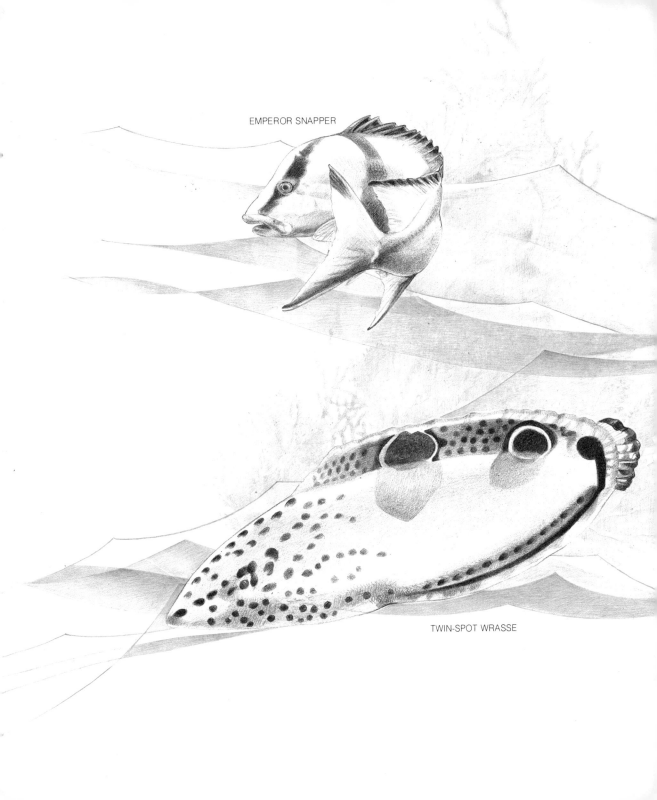

EMPEROR SNAPPER

TWIN-SPOT WRASSE

## Seen Only During Breeding

A fish that is camouflaged is well hidden from its enemies. It is also hidden from others of its own kind. For most of the year it makes little difference if fish of the same kind can see each other or not. But during the breeding season the males and females must be able to find each other if they are to lay eggs and produce babies. Some fishes become very brightly colored only during the breeding season. And this can be dangerous because they are more likely to be seen and eaten by their enemies.

There are two little fishes from streams in the central part of the United States that become colorful only during the breeding season. The red-bellied dace is a green-colored fish. Usually they have black lines and a yellowish line on their bodies. In the springtime, when they lay their eggs, both the male and the female dace get a fiery red color of the chin and all along the bottom side. With their bright red vest, the red-bellied dace is easily seen by others.

40

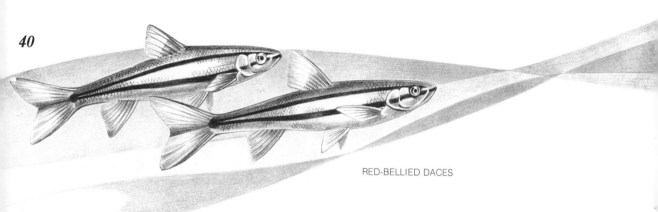

RED-BELLIED DACES

For most of the year, the rainbow darter is a plain green fish with slight coloring on its fins. During the breeding season, however, the body is covered with blue and red spots. The fins on the back become marked with bright blue, red and yellow. When it is at its brightest, the rainbow darter is one of the most colorful fish found in the United States.

RAINBOW DARTERS

WRASSE

GRAMMA

ROCK BEAUTY

BLENNY

PICASSO BUTTERFLY FISH

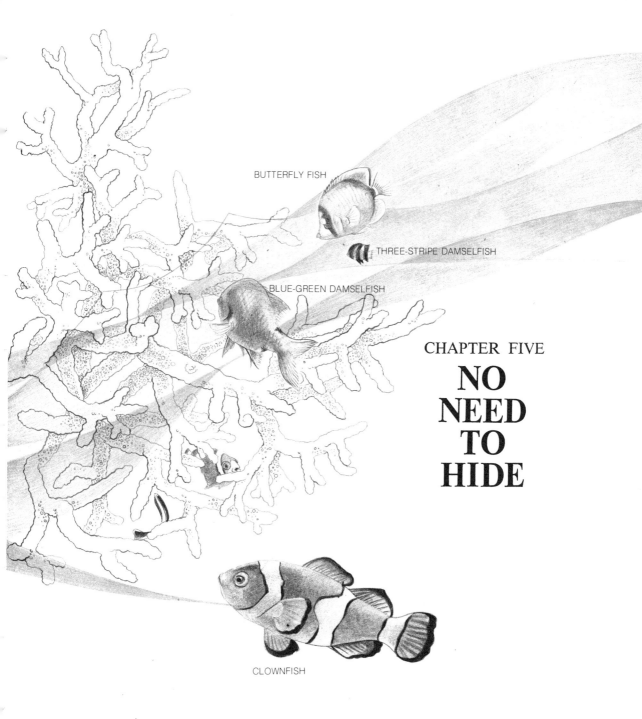

BUTTERFLY FISH

THREE-STRIPE DAMSELFISH

BLUE-GREEN DAMSELFISH

CHAPTER FIVE

# NO
# NEED
# TO
# HIDE

CLOWNFISH

There are many kinds of fishes that for one reason or another do not need to be camouflaged.

In several parts of the world there are fishes that live in streams that run through caves. Far inside, the caves are in total darkness. There are no enemies to harm these fishes. Cave fishes are always bright pink all over. Out in the sunlight they would be quickly eaten. But in the dark caves, it is not necessary to hide. The blind cave tetra from Mexico is often kept in home aquariums. It has no eyes, but it manages to swim around and find food.

Some of the most brightly colored fishes in the world are found around coral reefs. Some are blue, others are red and still others are yellow or orange. Many kinds are marked with two or more colors. Some are so bright that they shine like jewels. Coral fishes like these have no need to be camouflaged because the coral reefs are full of small holes. Whenever an enemy chases a coral fish, it darts into a hole where the enemy cannot catch it.

44

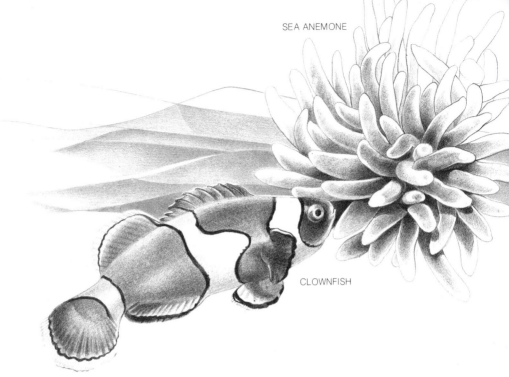

CLOWNFISH

One small reef fish from the South Pacific Ocean is so brightly marked that it is called the "clownfish." The clownfish is bright orange with broad white bands. It is easily seen and is just the right size and shape to make a tasty meal for many fishes. But the clownfish has a good friend for protection. It lives near another animal called a sea anemone. This animal has many long arms that are covered with stingers. Fishes that touch a sea anemone receive many painful stings; any fish but the clownfish, that is. The sea anemone never stings its "friend." Whenever the clownfish is attacked, it swims into the sea anemone's arms for protection. The clownfish's bright markings are a warning: "Attack me and you will be stung by my friend." Usually an enemy goes after a clownfish only once. From then on it stays away.

# CONCLUSION

By now you may be wondering how so many fishes came to have so many different kinds of camouflage. Scientists *think* they know the answer.

Fishes have been living in the waters of the Earth for many millions of years. Every once in a while a fish is born with different markings or different colors or a different shape than its parents, brothers and sisters. Usually this fish dies or is eaten by larger fishes. But suppose these markings help it to hide more easily from its enemies and it grows up. When it is old enough to have babies there is a good chance that some of them will have the same markings as the parent. So you see, changes that tend to help a fish live will often be kept and passed on to the young. Scientists believe that many of these changes have occurred in all kinds of animals over millions of years.

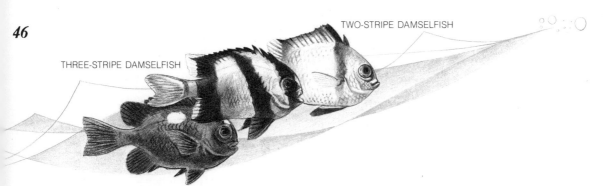

TWO-STRIPE DAMSELFISH

THREE-STRIPE DAMSELFISH

THREE-SPOT DAMSELFISH

# INDEX

## THE AUTHOR

*Alan Mark Fletcher's* knowledge of his subjects is first-hand: he has made at least ten expeditions into the South American jungle to study fishes and to gather materials for his writings. He spent nine years as editor of *The Aquarium,* a monthly hobby magazine, and has been a senior science editor with two major commercial publishers. A biology graduate of Juaniata College, Mr. Fletcher has also taught junior and senior high school science and is the author of six books for children. At present he is Science Editor of the Cornell University Press. He lives in Ithaca, New York, with his wife and four daughters.

## THE ARTIST

*Jean Day Zallinger* is a sensitive artist with many children's books to her credit. She formerly used her talents to illustrate *The Mayfly* by Ross E. Hutchins. In *Fishes That Hide,* she has again lent beauty and charm to an Addison-Wesley book with her delicate renderings of the underwater life of fishes. A mother of three, Mrs. Zallinger is a graduate of Yale's School of Fine Arts.

WITHDRAWN